Your Money

Your Money

A Biblical Guide
To Personal Money Management

George and MarJean Fooshee

A Barbour Book

Scripture quotations identified NIV are taken from the *Holy Bible, New International Version®*, NIV®, © 1973, 1978, 1984 by the International Bible Society. Used by permission of Zondervan Publishing House. All rights reserved.

Scripture quotations identified TLB are from *The Living Bible*, © 1971. Used by permission of Tyndale House Publishers, Inc., Wheaton, IL 60189. All rights reserved.

Scripture quotations identified RSV are from the *Revised Standard Version of The Bible*, © 1946, 1952, 1971 by the Division of Christian Education of the National Council of the Churches of Christ in the USA. Used by permission.

Scripture quotations identified NAS are from the *New American Standard Bible*, © 1960, 1962, 1963, 1968, 1971, 1972, 1973, 1975, 1977 by The Lockman Foundation. Used by permission.

ISBN 1-55748-458-9

Published by Barbour and Company, Inc., P.O. Box 719, Uhrichsville, Ohio 44683.

Material for *Your Money* is taken from *You Can Be Financially Free* and *You Can Beat the Money Squeeze* by George Fooshee.

Printed in the United States of America.

Contents

Acknowledgment

The publisher would like to acknowledge the generous help of Jackie Inglehard, editor of *The Penny Pincher* newsletter, in supplying material for "199 Ways to Save Money."

Preface

The phones keep ringing! The letters keep coming! "May I come see you? I've got troubles!" Voices desperate, tight, worried. People with money problems, fearful, pressured, SQUEEZED.

By the world's standards, we in America today are rich, yet we're poor. Families are squirming, with parents bringing home insufficient money to pay the bills and hack at the debts.

How did we get this way? How can we get UNSQUEEZED?

Explore scriptural principles like the ones below. You'll see how the Bible can keep you from being squeezed and show you how to get unsqueezed:

- Get the facts.
- Stay out of debt.
- Keep records.
- Spend sensibly.

This book will deal with these principles in a number of ways. We'll discuss debts, cars, housing, and other topics. We'll try to present clearly and simply from the Scriptures the principles God has established for money. The Bible speaks specifically, for example, about:

- *Sharing:* "For if you give, you will get! ..." (Luke 6:38 TLB).

- *Spending:* ". . . be content with what you have. . . ." (Hebrews 13:5 RSV).

- *Saving:* "The wise man saves for the future. . . ." (Proverbs 21:20 TLB).

7

To help you practically, we'll answer many questions people have asked about finances. And we have an added special feature that looks like this:

Marjean's 2¢: To Help You Get Unsqueezed
My wife Marjean will offer you some sage advice from her own experiences on the various topics through this format. She has shared my vision for Christians to be financially free, has encouraged me in my ministry, and has worked with me in the finances of our marriage. These little asides have an important contribution to make to this book.

Why all this emphasis on money for the Christian? Since the Bible speaks about money so often, the Christian must listen. To be in harmony with God — to receive the blessings He has for us and to be used for His good purposes — we Christians must know and obey God's money principles.

If you are not a Christian, you still can profit from an awareness of clear financial principles. Decisions about money matters have far-reaching and cumulative effects on your present lifestyle as well as on your future choices. Some decisions now may save you thousands of dollars in your lifetime — dollars which may have great meaning to your family during a crisis or an opportunity.

Knowledge of and obedience to God's money principles frequently are lacking. Ask any minister how often money worries arise in marital counseling. My own experience indicates financial pressures and tensions exist in most marriages. Many couples would rather be mired in debt than face the trauma of working through to agreement on the family budget and then keeping records to check their progress. Singles fail just as easily in their money management, with the resultant crop of frustration and despair.

God's Way is the "narrow gate" that is hard, but His Way leads to *abundant life*. The world's way in money is the easy payment way — so easy and wide — but it leads to destruction! The fruits of the easy way are bills, payments, interest, pressure, and financial bondage. As one minister who was trying to climb up the long trail out of debt wrote, "We are getting our debts whittled down, but it sure is slower than it was getting into them." Many of you who read this book will be able to shout "Amen" to that!

Why look to the Bible for information about installment loans, revolving charge accounts, mortgage payments, budgeting, investments, and the intricacies of personal finances? Aren't these financial complexities all products of a modern credit system developed long after the Bible was written?

Not really. The easy payment methods of going broke fast are relatively new, but God's established principles for money are timeless — and are as relevant today as His simple eternal message of salvation: "Repent, and believe in the gospel" (Mark 1:15 RSV).

In our financial seminars, we often ask people what goals they have for the day. The ones most frequently listed are these:

- To set up a household budget and stick to it.
- To be able to recognize the signs of getting into financial trouble, before the trouble gets too bad.
- To learn how to be good stewards and use sound principles to manage all that God has given us.
- To learn how to pass these principles on to our children so they can begin now to manage well.
- To learn how to save more money.
- To know how to get out of debt.
- To be financially free and better use what income God has allowed us to earn.
- To learn how to manage money so that it is not wasted.

Almost everyone who comes to us for financial counseling wants to reach some or all of these goals. You're probably reading this book in order to reach such goals. This book was written to help you avoid the financial squeeze and become and stay financially free, to the glory of God. Our prayer is that you will learn and apply these financial principles to your life so that you will experience God's best in the wise use of your money.

1: Dealing With Debt's Deadly Squeeze

Have you ever seen smoking listed as one of the leading reasons for divorce? Have you read that someone committed suicide and left a note saying that smoking was the cause of his despondency? Probably not! But you may be familiar with the label that's always included with cigarette ads: WARNING! THE USE OF THIS PRODUCT MAY BE INJURIOUS TO YOUR HEALTH.

You may be using an item that contains no such warning label from the Treasurer of the United States. Look at your credit cards. Do you see anywhere on them any warnings such as these?

> Warning! The use of this product may cause tension in your marriage. It may make you irritable. It could lead to severe depression. It could cost you a job opportunity. It may enslave you forever. It may, in the future, cause a drastic change in your lifestyle.

On many credit cards, however, this true but seldom-noticed statement is printed on the back: "Customer by retaining or using this card agrees to be bound. . . ." Being caught in the debt trap is in great contrast to the purpose God has for our lives. "For I am the Lord your God who brought you out of the land of Egypt, with the intention that you be slaves no longer; I have broken your chains and will make you walk with dignity" (Leviticus 26:13 TLB). The result of credit card spending is usually the binding up of one's finances with a continual round of interest and payments that never seems to stop.

In addition to letting you charge purchases, credit card companies present you with so-called convenience checks. When you want to spend more than you have, you simply fill out your convenience check. Instantly you have secured what they call a cash advance. The check you have written has been an instant addition to your bank credit card account. You have borrowed that money at an annual percentage rate of 9 to 18 percent. This "easy solution," this "peace of mind" promised by the credit institutions, adds up to one word which the advertising neglects to mention: DEBT!

What's so bad about debt? Isn't everybody in hock? Don't companies owe money? Isn't virtually every city and state government liable for millions of dollars? Isn't our federal government constantly raising the legal debt limit a few more billion dollars? Aren't most churches involved in debt? What's the catch?

The catch is that debt is a *trap*.

The Debt Trap

The Bible expresses real caution about traps: "When a bird sees a trap being set, it stays away, but not these men; they trap themselves! They lay a booby trap for their own lives" (Proverbs 1:17, 18 TLB).

The characteristics of a trap are that it is:

• attractive
• easy to get into
• almost impossible to escape from

No wonder debt is called a trap. The characteristics of debt fit its definition so well.

Didn't Jesus tell us He came that we may have life and have it more abundantly (see John 10:10 KJV)? Doesn't the abundant life mean having what you want when you want it? Doesn't the abundant life mean new cars, wide-screen televisions, state-of-the-art home entertainment centers, several bathrooms and stylish clothes for each season?

Some families who have come to me for counseling have discovered the pitfalls of such abundance when the foundation for their possessions is built on debt. In this group were two ministers, one top executive, a salesman, a professional man and a divorcé. All

were Christians seeking a closer walk with Christ. Yet one man's job
was threatened because of his financial predicament. Another man
recently had been hospitalized for several days, having succumbed
emotionally to the debt pressures bearing upon him. Although these
six had incomes ranging from under $30,000 to more than $100,000
per year, they all had two things in common. They were all deeply in
debt, and they all had learned the reality of this little jingle:

> That money talks.
> I'll not deny.
> I heard it once.
> It said, good-bye.

A Revealing Definition of Debt

What is debt? A usual definition is that *debt* is something owed to
another. There is a sense of obligation on the part of the borrower to
pay back the debt to the lender. The word *lend* means to let another
have or use for a time. When the time is up, the money is expected
to be repaid. In the meantime, the borrower is living in a second state
— the state of debt. Now he's a member of the "debt set."

Why do those who sell easy credit fail to use the word *debt* in
their ads? Why are the adjectives commonly used for debt left out of
descriptions of the new state into which you move when you borrow
money? When I looked at all the adjectives listed for debt in *Roget's
College Thesaurus*, I quickly understood the reasons:

> indebted; liable, chargeable, answerable for, in debt, in embar-
> rassed circumstances; in difficulties; encumbered, involved;
> involved in debt, plunged in debt; deep in debt; deeply in-
> volved; up against it; in the red; fast tied up; insolvent; minus,
> out of pocket; unpaid; unrequited, unrewarded; owing, due, in
> arrears, outstanding. *Slang*, in hock, on the cuff.

Were you uncomfortable as you saw this list? Did you notice the
negative aspects of each word and phrase used to describe *debt*?

Debt, in God's economy, is an excess of liabilities over assets.

A home, if financed conservatively, usually may be sold for more than is owed by the mortgagor. A car, furniture, or most any depreciating item purchased on time cannot usually be sold for sufficient money to pay off the lender. Ask any credit union or bank how they come out financially when goods are repossessed. My experience is that repossession is usually a financial disaster for both the borrower and the lender.

A good rule for borrowing is: Never borrow to buy depreciating items. Such things as cars, furniture, clothes, appliances, boats and luxury items should not be purchased until money is available to pay for them.

The family home is a special situation and will be considered in another chapter.

Three Reasons to Avoid Debt

God does not want His people in bondage: "And you will know the truth, and the truth will set you free" (John 8:32 TLB). God, always so positive, gives three reasons for avoiding debt:

1. Debt violates God's commandment for our lives. "Keep out of debt altogether . . ." (Romans 13:8 PHILLIPS). God says KEEP OUT! The sign is clear. Keeping out of debt certainly isn't easy.

Individuals I know in the debt trap took exactly the same road to get there: They spent more money than they made. They violated the principle to be content with their wages by overspending their income.

The Talmud has wise counsel for our spending: "A man should always eat and drink less than his means allow, clothe himself in accordance with his means, and honour his wife and children more than his means allow."

2. Debt is costly. Why are so many people blind to the pitfalls of easy credit? They do not count *the cost.* The Bible instructs: "But don't begin until you count the cost. For who would begin construction of a building without first getting estimates and then checking to see if he has enough money to pay the bills?" (Luke 14:28 TLB).

Most people are aware of the scriptural principle that you reap what you sow. The crop reaped from debt is *interest*.

3. Freedom is lost. "Just as the rich rule the poor, so the borrower is servant to the lender" (Proverbs 22:7 TLB). The person in debt is in bondage to his creditors. A portion of his pay is committed to pay back the debt; choices as to how to spend his pay are lost. A share of his possessions usually is pledged to assure repayment; the sale of these pledged possessions is not possible without the creditor's permission. Such freedom usually is not granted unless the creditor is paid in full, a situation which is seldom possible from the proceeds of the sale of the mortgaged property.

Other freedoms also are involved. I've noticed that money borrowed with a smile usually is paid back with a scowl. Debt is often a thief of joy. But I've seen hundreds experience the relief and joy that come when they've allowed God to lead them out of the debt trap. They've taken to heart God's message: "Evil men borrow and 'cannot pay it back!' But the good man returns what he owes with some extra besides" (Psalm 37:21 TLB).

The Pitfalls of Easy Credit

Our local newspaper once summed up the debt trap in a dramatic headline: "Easy Credit Way to Financial Hell."

Let's look at the easy part of credit. All that is required is to say, "Charge it," or to hand over a plastic card. What could be simpler? No money changes hands. You don't even have to think much about the cost of what you've spent.

My own experience with families is that if they're not keeping records, they're overspending. One man reported to me that when he finally decided to tally up his consumer debts, he was astounded to find he owed more than $35,000 as a result of constant overspending. The following tables will show you the result of credit card mania. Would you have any trouble spending $80 more than you make each month? The Debt Addition table shows what adding $80 a month, or $960 a year, to your debt will total in just five years at a compound interest rate of 18 percent.

Debt Addition

Year	Debt addition	Interest	Total debt
1	$ 960	$ 173	$1,133
2	$ 960	$ 377	$2,470
3	$ 960	$ 617	$4,047
4	$ 960	$ 901	$5,908
5	$ 960	$1,236	$8,104

Remember the warning that isn't on your credit card? The one the store does not issue on its revolving charge account: "The use of this card may cause a drastic change in your lifestyle!"

To repay an $8,000 debt in approximately the same length of time it took to accumulate it, at $960 per year, takes an annual payment of $2,438 per year. You can be out of debt in five years at the $2,438-per-year repayment.

Debt Repayment

Year	Debt addition	Interest	Total debt
1	$2,438	$1,350	$6,912
2	$2,438	$1,142	$5,616
3	$2,438	$ 894	$4,047
4	$2,438	$ 582	$2,216
5	$2,438	$ 222	—

What has the debt accumulation of $960 per year for five years cost?

Interest first five years	$3,304
Interest last five years	$4,190
Total interest	$7,494

The $960 debt accumulated each year for five years cost you an average annual interest of $749 for the 10-year period. And that's the cost in money.

But note the cost in trauma. Here's the situation. To go $80 per month into debt, the family simply refused to live within its income. Now, to escape the trap, they must take the following two dramatic, lifestyle-changing actions:

1. They must stop overspending $80 a month. Having said yes to spending and debt, they now must learn to say no to debt, go on a cash-only plan, and do without the $80 each month they used in credit.

2. The repayment of borrowing plus interest will require another dramatic change in lifestyle — an additional $203.15 per month. To pay off the $8,000 accumulated in five years of overspending, the $203.15 payment will need to be made for the next five years. Adding the two reductions in spendable income ($80 + $203.15) produces a $283.15 monthly change in their standard of living. In my experience, not many folks are able to do it. But God is a God of hope and One who helps us do it.

The Debt Set

Banks are making debt so easy that a whole new type of checking account has become common in modern America. This "miracle account" has been called an overdraft account, reserve account, balance-plus checking, and money management. These accounts enable you to plunge into debt simply by writing checks for more money than you have in your account. Suddenly, you've been loaned money (usually in $50 increments) to cover the overdraft. And you didn't have to fill out papers with all sorts of embarrassing questions about your income, debts, and other personal finances.

Christmas in America has become a season of much commercial ballyhoo. Advertisements hawk "a gift that forever solves the 'What to give?' problem. . . . The perfect gift for everyone. . . . A better gift than cash." And credit card companies obligingly promise, "You pay for it at your convenience."

When I see such sales tactics, my heart grieves. So many people believe credit cards, charge accounts, and overdraft accounts can solve their gift problems, make Christmas a joy, and forever solve their money woes. But God has such a clear, specific formula for paycheck management. The Bible says "make do with your pay!" (Luke 3:14 NEB). The violation of this checkbook formula transforms the Debt Set into the Debtor Set.

Marjean's 2¢: Marjean's Super Gift

How thrilled I was when I received a box of hand-painted notecards with my initials, flowers, and cute little animal caricatures. These notes were drawn lovingly on a pad of plain paper by a close friend. I very carefully selected them to send to special people who would appreciate the individually decorated notes.

The same idea could be adapted by buying an inexpensive pad of paper and package of envelopes. Decorate them with pictures carefully cut out of old greeting cards or magazines and pasted on the front of the folded note paper. Or, if you happen to be artistic (try your hand), decorate the notes with some marking pens.

Anyone would be thrilled to receive such a personalized gift. Any number of ideas for practical and inexpensive gifts are available. Try your creativity, have fun, and save money!

A Trap Within a Trap: Cosigning

The world offers another sneaky way of plunging a person into the debt trap. This sinister method is called *cosigning*. People who cosign feel they are doing a relative or friend a favor. The potential cost of their signature usually is not explained very carefully to them. In a given situation, the cosigner may feel some embarrassment at quizzing the lender about what will happen if this relative or friend does not pay as promised.

The Scriptures warn us to avoid cosigning:

> Son, if you endorse a note for someone you hardly know, guaranteeing his debt, you are in serious trouble. You may have trapped yourself by your agreement. Quick! Get out of it if you possibly can! Swallow your pride; don't let embarrassment stand in the way. Go and beg to have your name erased. Don't put it off. Do it now. Don't rest until you do. If you can get out of this trap you have saved yourself like a deer that escapes from a hunter, or a bird from the net.
> *Proverbs 6:1-5 TLB*

Let me explain what you are doing if you cosign a note. I want you to understand the financial transaction in which you would involve yourself. Here are three steps:

1. *You are borrowing the money.* The lender has refused to make the loan to the person for whom you are cosigning. His decision has been based on facts which reveal that the risk is too great to loan the money to your friend or relative. When you sign the note, the money is really being loaned to you. The reason you have been asked to sign is because your collateral, your character, your credit, and your capacity are sufficient for him to feel good about his security on the loan. Your signature is his security.

2. *You are loaning the money you borrowed to a person who was too great a risk for the professional lender.* You are involving yourself in a business transaction the expert money manager wouldn't touch.

3. *You are hoping your friend or relative will pay back the loan.*
I can tell you he probably won't. My friends who are bankers tell me
that approximately 50 percent of all cosigners end up paying. One
financial publication has stated that 80 percent of all cosigners have
to pay back those notes they cosigned. Bitterness is often the result.

When your friend or relative defaults, then you have the
"privilege" of paying back the money. It's been my experience that
cosigners seldom plan on this repayment. I also have witnessed much
bitterness in the lives of people over the repayment of such agree-
ments. One of the reasons God counsels us against cosigning, I
believe, is because of the destructive potential in a human relationship
that often results from this kind of financial transaction.

Whenever you cosign you are violating God's commandment to
keep out of debt. You have assumed the debt of another. That's just
another way to enter the state of debt.

"Forgive Us Our Debts"

Our Lord's Prayer contains the well-known, often-prayed phrase
"... forgive us our debts. ..." (Matthew 6:12 KJV). Our government
and the vast majority of Americans act as though the simple utterance
of that phrase erases the penalty of past borrowing and allows them
to go right on overspending. The astronomical growth of the federal
debt in recent years demonstrates how, collectively, we are failing to
be content with our wages.

2: Escaping the Debt Trap

Have you ever skied?

Zooming down the slopes is exhilarating. Climbing up without a lift is a different story. You would not knowingly ski where the lifts are not functioning.

Zooming into debt is also exciting. However, the price of escaping the trap is greater than most people realize.

As we suggested in the last chapter, simply to stop overspending is not enough. A *triple financial reverse* is involved.

Look at these steps which must be taken in order to work out of the debt trap:

1. *Stop spending more than you make!*
2. *Repay the debts!*
3. *Pay the interest!*

If an unsuspecting spender has been blowing $1,000 more each year than he makes, his first step must be to stop that practice. Changing his habit of overspending will not be easy. He may agree with the fellow who said most of us would be delighted to pay as we go if we could just catch up with paying as we've gone!

If you think that's hard, visualize his efforts to eliminate the debt without further borrowing: He must make payments on the principal *and* continue to pay interest. The figures in the following table reveal the hard road of payments ahead to eliminate the debt of $10,000 accumulated in 10 years of overspending, at a 10-percent annual interest rate. Assume the family paid off $1,000 each year on their debt — in addition to paying the interest.

Cost of Debt Payment

Year	Payment	Interest	Balance due ($10,000)
1	$ 2,000	$1,000	$9,000
2	1,900	900	8,000
3	1,800	800	7,000
4	1,700	700	6,000
5	1,600	600	5,000
6	1,500	500	4,000
7	1,400	400	3,000
8	1,300	300	2,000
9	1,200	200	1,000
10	1,100	100	. . . . .
Total	$15,500	———	———

What did it cost to accumulate $10,000 of debt over 10 years at a 10-percent interest rate? What was the interest cost during a repayment period of 10 years?

Interest first 10 years	$5,500
Interest last 10 years	$5,500
Total interest	$11,000
Average annual interest, 20 years	$550

What a price to pay for the temporary pleasure of overspending each paycheck! Do you see clearly what it means to work for your money? Do you understand why "easy payments" now make most people uneasy later?

The combination of change from overspending $1,000 per year to reducing expenses by $1,550 (in order to meet the average payment) is a $2,550-per-year change in a living standard. Few people ever make the effort. Hundreds of thousands of Americans every year are resorting to personal bankruptcy rather than making the effort to repay their debts.

However, Jesus said, "What is impossible with men is possible with God" (Luke 18:27 RSV). Escaping the debt trap to the glory of God is a tremendous objective. Here are the steps to help you work out your own plan of escape:

1. *Set a goal.*
2. *Start giving a set percentage of your income to the Lord.*
3. *List all you owe and all you own.*
4. *Have a sale.*
5. *Fix a monthly debt payment amount.*
6. *Add no new debts.*
7. *Establish a time goal.*
8. *Cut the goal in half.*
9. *Develop a repayment schedule.*
10. *Share the repayment schedule with your creditors.*
11. *Stick to your plan.*

Your journey to financial freedom must necessarily be an individual one. Your own circumstances will have a lot to say about your plan. The steps discussed here can serve as a guide to map out your own course. A brief explanation will help you understand its simplicity as well as their usefulness.

1. Set a goal. One of my friends says he would rather aim at something and miss it than aim at nothing and hit it. Deciding to get out of debt is the very first step.

Think for a minute about the benefits of getting out of debt. Such action will reduce your expenses, delight your creditors, provide financial freedom, and please God. Such benefits provide excellent motivation for setting a goal of paying all your debts. Since a clear goal will put you out in front of 95 people out of every 100, you are well on your way to becoming debt-free.

Incidentally, I've never seen anyone get out of debt by accident.

2. Start giving a set percentage of your income to the Lord. Most Christians abandon their giving along the path into the debt trap. People reason that it does not make sense to give money away when there is not enough to pay the bills. God says, "But seek first his kingdom and his righteousness, and all these things shall be yours as well" (Matthew 6:33 RSV). In my opinion, "seeking first" means giving the first part of your income to the Lord.

Do you want God's blessing stamped on your get-out-of-debt project? Then don't be foolish and keep going into debt with God. I've seen many try it, but no one succeeds. Start giving a set percentage of your income out of each paycheck.

3. *List all you owe and all you own.* It may be difficult to believe, but most people don't have a good grasp of what they owe. A listing of all your debts, with the monthly payments required and the annual percentage rates of interest, can be most helpful. The headings on the "What We Owe" list would look like this: **Who We Owe, Total Amount Due, Monthly Payment, Interest Rate**, and **Percent of Total Debt**.

Now list "What We Own." This list would include most of the things bought with borrowed money. Such items as automobiles, furniture, appliances, your home, and luxury objects might be some of what you own.

Take a good look at both lists. Under "What We Owe," did you include any amounts due relatives? I find that people frequently neglect to put family loans on their lists, feeling they don't have to be repaid. Put them on your list. They certainly are part of what you owe.

Have you included everything you own — musical instruments, collections, guns, sports equipment, and hobby items?

4. *Have a sale.* Study the list of things you own. Which of these *can* you do without? (Notice I didn't say "*want* to do without.") Most people have no idea of what they can do without until they try. One couple who counseled with me recently discovered they could eliminate 20 percent of their total debt by selling one car. They were able to apply the amount of that car payment to further debt reduction. Don't think about how much you will lose of what you paid for the item you are selling. Think how much you will gain, which can be applied to your debt reduction immediately.

Your attitude about things will determine your success in working your way out of the debt trap. I remember a young woman who came to me for counseling. Her finances were a mess. There were insufficient funds to cover a string of checks she had written. Her car payments were three months past due. Many charge accounts were delinquent. Creditors were after her constantly.

As we gathered the facts about her finances, I saw the difficulty of her continuing to make car payments and operate an automobile. "Could you get along without your car?" I asked her. Her reply was so quick it surprised me. "Impossible!" she exclaimed.

With the knowledge of the following facts, I failed to see the impossibility of her getting along without a car: 1) She lived within easy walking distance of work, and bus transportation was very convenient; 2) some neighbors and fellow employees had offered her rides to and from work and church; 3) shopping was also convenient to her house.

With her attitude, however, it was really impossible to clear up her financial plight. Within a few weeks she had lost her job because of repercussions from her personal financial irresponsibility.

5. *Set a monthly debt payment amount.* You will have to squeeze this money out of your monthly income. Now divide this figure into the total amount you owe, to arrive at the number of months it will take you to be debt-free. Interest will add slightly to the time schedule, but the answer you get gives you the minimum amount of time for your debt repayment plan.

6. *Add no new debts.* You must decide once and for all that you will not borrow money for any reason or charge any items. This would be an excellent time to have a credit card destruction ceremony in your home. Gather your family around, take a large pair of scissors, and deliberately cut each credit card into tiny pieces. Make a list of all charge accounts. Call or write each store and tell them to close your account. You cannot work your way out of debt if you continue to add new borrowings.

The key to your success in avoiding new debt will be to *do without.* You will be amazed at all the so-called necessities you can learn to do without. Some of our friends made all sorts of interesting discoveries during their journey out of debt. Their story is told by Marjean on page 65 of this book. Not only could they do without; they found their lives were enriched by making do. You, too, will be in for some exciting revelations as you learn to do without.

7. *Establish a time goal.* Write down the number of months, according to your plan, it will take to become debt-free.

8. *Cut the goal in half.* That's right! If you have determined it will take you four years, or 48 months, to get out of debt, then write down a figure of one-half that time.

In view of your income and other financial obligations, you may think I've gone crazy. But let me give you a simple formula for cutting your debt repayment time in half.

What is the amount of money you plan to set aside each month for debt repayment? An examination of the Debt Pay-Off table will show you how long it will take you to pay off various amounts of debt with specific monthly payment amounts, assuming the money was borrowed at an annual interest rate of 12 percent.

Debt Pay-Off:
Monthly Payments at 12% Interest Rate

Debt amount	\(Years to pay off debt\) 1	2	3	4	5
$ 1,000	$ 88.85	$ 47.08	$ 33.2	$ 26.34	$ 22.25
2,000	177.70	94.15	66.43	52.67	44.49
3,000	266.55	141.23	99.65	79.01	66.64
4,000	355.40	188.30	132.86	105.34	88.98
5,000	444.25	235.37	166.08	131.67	111.23
6,000	533.10	282.45	199.29	158.01	133.47
7,000	621.95	329.52	232.51	184.34	155.72
8,000	710.80	376.59	265.72	210.68	177.96
9,000	799.64	423.67	298.93	237.01	200.21
10,000	888.49	470.74	332.15	263.34	222.45
12,000	1,066.19	564.89	398.58	316.01	266.94
14,000	1,243.89	659.03	465.01	368.68	311.43
16,000	1,421.59	753.18	531.43	421.35	355.92

Assume you have a $5,000 debt and you have set aside the $131.67 it will take each month to repay the debt in four years. To find the amount of monthly payment it will take to pay off the debt in half that time, look across the table beneath the two-year column. The monthly amount to pay off a $5,000 debt in two years, at a 12-percent interest rate, is $235.37.

Paying this debt in two years (24 months) at $235.37 monthly will cost you a total of $5,696.88. Taking four years (48 months) to pay back the same $5,000 debt at $131.67 monthly will cost you a total of $6,320.16. That's $623.28 more in interest costs — which should give you sufficient incentive to look hard at my plan for cutting your debt payment time in half.

Here's how you can do it. Subtract the $131.67 monthly payment from the $235.37 monthly payment; your monthly cost to pay off your debt in half the time is not twice $131.67, but only an additional $103.70. The only way I know to save money in paying off debts is to pay them off faster. The faster you pay, the less it costs.

"But," you ask, "how can we come up with $103.70 a month above our payment of $131.67? Haven't we pared our budget to the bare bone?"

You probably have. Your solution will depend on your family's creativity.

Again, let's look at the objective. The challenge is to cut your debt repayment time in half. Expressing this goal in positive terms would be to say you are going to get out of debt twice as fast as you had planned. To do that, you don't have to double your income or cut your expenses in half.

Let me challenge your thinking as to how to do it. Despite high unemployment in many areas, countless opportunities for income go begging because no one can be found to do the work. For example, consider domestic help. Yes, that's what I mean — house cleaning. Domestic help comes under the federal minimum wage law. The hourly minimum wage is $4.25. That's $34 for an eight-hour day. Maybe you don't want to perform that work. But working one day or two mornings a week could bring in more than enough to allow you to cut your debt repayment time in half.

An alternative could be to have the whole family clean a house one Saturday a month. If you could find a family in your neighborhood who wants their house cleaned and who would be willing to pay your whole family to do the job at a family hourly rate, investing this day to cut your debt repayment time in half would be a worthwhile family project.

Remember the door-to-door magazine salesman's familiar opening line, "I'm working my way through college?" Maybe your family slogan could be, "We're working our way out of debt."

Other family projects might involve baby-sitting or working for short-term projects of health foundations, organizational fund drives, or political campaigns. Many churches have difficulty finding volunteer help and are willing to pay for part-time jobs in the kitchen or nursery; some pay for part-time custodial help. To add $103.70 to your monthly income takes only $25.92 per week; at the $4.25 minimum wage, that's about six hours of work per week. With two family members working, it would take only a few hours a week.

Can you visualize a regular weekly project of working this amount of time together as a way of cutting out two years of debt repayment? If you have teen-agers, allowing them to have a part in the debt repayment program could be excellent training.

How can you find a place to sell your services and add extra income to move you out of the debt trap more quickly? People say they can't find anyone to do certain jobs these days. What are these jobs?

Try to find out. Ask people.

I've had a man and his wife clean my office for many years. They've done this three nights a week, after his regular work hours. This is when they get in their talk time. Finding dependable janitorial service is often a problem for small businesses that require cleaning only once or twice a week. Usually, the business will furnish the necessary equipment. Inquire of churches in your neighborhood; ask questions at the stores where you shop; ask around where you work. Keep your eyes open for lawns that need mowing or shrubs that need trimming, right in your own neighborhood. You'll be surprised how much you're worth if you're only willing to invest a few hours a week.

Imaginative ways to earn extra money are limited only by a lack of creativity and desire. Here are just a few ideas to stimulate your thinking:

Ushering at concerts or sporting events
Walking pets
Pet-sitting while owners are gone
Tutoring children in school work
Typing term papers
House-sitting, including plant care and security checks
Shoveling snow
Raking leaves, other yard work
Stripping wallpaper
Washing windows, washing cars
Painting (inside and out)
Cooking and clean-up when others entertain in their homes

Another way to hasten your escape from the debt trap is to agree in advance to add any extra income to debt repayment. This would include raises, bonuses, tax refunds, garage sale income, or any other unusual income that comes into your family.

9. Develop a repayment schedule. Usually, writing down your plan will help you achieve it. Use notebook paper, and allow enough space to include the number of months to fulfill your plan. The chart would begin like this:

Repayment schedule Creditor A	January	February	March
Payment planned			
Amount paid			
Balance due			

Continue with a listing of each creditor in the left column and add to the months according to your plan. Be sure to total the payments and the balance due.

Take the amount you owe off of the list you've made; divide it by the number of months you plan to take to get out of debt. Insert that figure in the "Payment Planned" row. At the end of each month, after you've made your payments, write down the amount paid and the balance due.

You also can keep a monthly total of the payments to all creditors and the balance due on all your debts at the end of each month. Recording your payments will give you a sense of satisfaction. Watching the balances diminish will give you an excitement that will help you stick to your goal.

10. *Take or send a copy of your repayment schedule to your creditors.* I promise you they will be very impressed with the fact that you have made out a plan. They will be even more impressed as you send them the regular monthly payment you have promised. Also tell them that if something happens to delay their payment, you will contact them ahead of the payment due date.

I have worked with hundreds of credit grantors. I have yet to find one who will not go along with a person who makes an honest effort to pay some amount regularly on his or her bill. It is rare to find a creditor who will turn an account over to a collection agency when the debtor has communicated in advance of missing a promised payment.

11. *Stick to your plan.* You'll be tempted again and again to quit. Don't do it! Each missed payment will set you back on your goal. The devil uses simple tools like these to keep you from escaping the debt trap to the glory of God: "It won't hurt to miss the debt payment this month — after all, it's December." Or, "Why bother to keep all those records. . . ?"

Starting something is easier than finishing. More people start the race than finish. Life is littered with drop-outs who quit when the going gets rough. The Bible has a very specific word of encouragement as you escape the debt trap: "Having started the ball rolling so enthusiastically, you should carry this project through to completion just as gladly, giving whatever you can out of whatever you have. Let your enthusiastic idea at the start be equalled by your realistic action now" (2 Corinthians 8:11 TLB).

Escaping the debt trap will require persistence. Some new attitudes about your way of living will be essential. Huffing and puffing with your money must be replaced by a different way of financial breathing — living on a margin.

3: Living On a Margin

Do you arrive at places on time?

Are you usually early?

Are you frequently late?

If your experience is similar to mine, you find that it is difficult if not impossible for most of us to arrive at places exactly on time. We are usually early or late. Our habits are well established; the early bird is consistent, and the late arrivers are regularly late.

I did some thinking about my own pattern of going places. In all honesty, I can say my usual arrival at appointments averaged five minutes past the starting time. Look at how this affected me over a 16-year period:

365 days x 16 years = 5,840 days in 16 years

5,840 x 3 average appointments/day = 17,520 appointments

17,520 x 5 minutes late = 87,600 minutes late
1,460 hours late
61 days late
2 months late

You may be astounded to see, as I was, that during those 16 years my five minutes of being late added up to two full months of 24-hour days.

In thinking about arriving late, I realized the two months of late minutes were greatly overshadowed by the fact that for each time I was five minutes late, I spent about 15 minutes *hurrying to be late*.

I believe you should take care of your body. That's just good

30

stewardship. Consequently, each week I try to swim, jog, or ride a bike at least five times. This works off accumulated tensions and helps keep my body in physical condition. The medical experts tell me exercise is a great preventive, when it comes to heart attacks.

Everything I read about the heart states tension is one of the leading killers. What a revelation! During those 16 years, I had spent an additional six months of 24-hour days pushing, rushing, pressing, and straining while hurrying to arrive five minutes late. It also seemed true in my case that when hurrying to be late, circumstances often occurred which put me under additional pressures and caused me to be even later — and certainly more tense.

Another observation is that after I had arrived some place late, I was angry with myself, self-centered, and seldom mentally prepared to participate in the situation for which I had hurried to be late.

In a radio program titled "Start Late, Stay Late," Earl Nightingale summed it up this way: "When you start late, it seems all the forces on earth conspire to further delay you." If you start late, you just never catch up. Nightingale continued, "One of the most important lessons a person can learn, in my opinion, is to start early. It can probably even add years to his life span. When you start early, everything goes great, nothing ever seems to go wrong, and the whole day is better for it. You're relaxed, smiling, and comfortable."

While pondering my own bad habits in this area, I had lunch with a man who is an elder in our church. As I drove downtown to pick him up — late, of course — the thought struck me that John was always early for appointments. I was confident he would be on the corner earlier than the time we had set. When he got into the car, I asked him, "John, how do you manage to arrive every place early?"

He replied with a question to me, "When do you plan to arrive?" My answer was that I tried to be there just on time. "That's your problem," John said. "You've got to operate on a margin and plan to get there early."

Instantly I learned a valuable lesson. I started allowing at least a 5 to 10-minute margin in my time plans. Going places now is almost like being on vacation. There is time to observe the sights, hear the sounds, smell the smells, and still arrive in a relaxed frame of mind. Living on a *time margin* has done wonders for my health and my attitude. Earl Nightingale was right; so was John.

Living on a *financial margin* has attractive benefits, too. Since there are only three ways to handle your income, you have a choice. You can save money, which is operating on a financial margin. You can break even, which is spending exactly what you make. Or you can go into debt, which is spending more than you make. Plunging into debt, overspending your income, is arriving late with your money.

Solomon tells us, "The wise man saves for the future, but the foolish man spends whatever he gets" (Proverbs 21:20 TLB). Saving money makes us wise in God's sight. Furthermore, saving money produces exciting economic rewards.

Let's assume you decide to live on a modest margin and save $1,000 per year. What happens if you save that much of your income and receive six-percent interest, compounded annually, for 10 years?

The table below shows the advantages of the financial margin.

Growth of Savings (6% Interest)

Year	Amount	Interest earned	Ending balance
1	$ 1,000	$ 60.00	$ 1,060.00
2	1,000	123.60	2,183.60
3	1,000	191.02	3,374.62
4	1,000	262.48	4,637.10
5	1,000	338.23	5,975.33
6	1,000	418.52	7,393.85
7	1,000	503.63	8,897.48
8	1,000	593.85	10,491.33
9	1,000	689.48	12,180.81
10	1,000	790.85	13,971.66
Total	$10,000	$3,971.66	$13,971.66

Planned Withdrawals

Year	Amount	Interest earned	Ending balance
11	$ 2,000	$ 718.30	$12,689.96
12	2,000	641.40	11,331.36
13	2,000	559.88	9,891.24
14	2,000	473.47	8,364.71
15	2,000	381.88	6,746.59
16	2,000	284.80	5,031.39
17	2,000	181.88	3,213.27
18	2,000	72.80	1,286.07
19	1,286	. . . . .	
Total	$17,286	$3,314.41	

Are you amazed to see that the $10,000 saved has increased to $13,972 because of compound interest? By saving $1,000 at six-percent interest during each of 10 years, you are able to withdraw $2,000 per year for eight years, or a total of $16,000, and still have $1,286 left in your account.

Can you grasp the staggering differences between saving money — arriving early — versus being late with your income? The dollar differences are amazing. Living on a margin results in interest additions to your money of $3,972.

In the previous chapter we described a borrower who was late with his income and borrowed at 10-percent interest; this cost $5,500 — and he still had a 10-year accumulated debt to repay.

While withdrawing your savings over the succeeding years, you will earn an additional $3,314 in interest. During the period of planned savings and withdrawal, your savings will earn a total of $7,286 interest. By contrast, for the period of debt accumulation *and* repayment in our previous example, the interest costs were $11,000. There is a whopping $18,286 difference between living on a margin versus choosing the debt trap way.

There are two types of people: those who work for their money and those who have their money work for them. Which type would you choose to be?

God commends the ant for its wisdom in following the savings principle: "There are . . . things that are small but unusually wise: Ants aren't strong, but store up food for the winter. . . ." (Proverbs 30:24 TLB).

4: Squeezing Through Inflation

Although inflation has not been a headline grabber in the early '90s, economic price increases are a historical fact. The low three-percent average increase in the Consumer Price Index in the early '90s seemed like nothing compared to much higher increases in the '70s and '80s. Even historical low rates will affect the prices of what you buy, future college costs, and living expenses, and your retirement planning.

Inflation raises two difficult questions: 1) How does one plan for or handle inflation? 2) Saving sounds great, but with inflation a known fact, don't we lose money by saving it, instead of being in debt and paying back later with cheaper money?

As Christians, we face choices in our money management. Will we handle our money the world's way or the biblical way?

Some ideas from a recent book that suggest ways to fight inflation include: 1) Avoid paying your bills for as long as possible; 2) Don't be ashamed to flirt on the ragged edge of being a dead beat.

The world's way is to borrow all you can on things that will cost more later. As inflation accelerates, you pay back the loans with cheaper dollars.

Early in 1979 an American businessman in England filed the largest personal bankruptcy ever recorded, until that time: $209 million. He had followed the borrow-on-property strategy to beat inflation and get rich. He got into trouble when he was unable to pay off his debts, because unexpected things happened that affected his income.

Lifestyles For These Times

God's way, on the other hand, involves these principles:
   1. Recognize God as the owner of all we have. The whole world

is His! We are only stewards, managers and caretakers of it: ". . . For all the world is mine, and everything in it. . . . I want you to trust me in your times of trouble, so I can rescue you, and you can give me glory" (Psalm 50:12, 15 TLB).

2. *Live as a giver.* Whatever we have, God wants us to return a portion to Him, in recognition that we acknowledge His ownership and trust Him.

The best guarantee against inflation I've found in the Bible is in Malachi 3, an often-quoted chapter on giving. After we're told to be givers, the prophet gives us this promise from God:

> "Your crops will be large, for I will guard them from insects and plagues. Your grapes won't shrivel away before they ripen," says the Lord of Hosts. "And all nations will call you blessed, for you will be a land sparkling with happiness. These are the promises of the Lord of Hosts." *Malachi 3:11, 12 TLB*

Inflation eats away at the value of our money just as insects and plagues eat away at crops. Handling money God's way enables Him to guard the resources I manage for Him.

3. *Live as a saver.* The ant is singled out in Scripture for special mention because of storing up food for the winter (Proverbs 30:24, 25). The ant is a saver. Solomon said the wise man is a saver, but the fool spends all his money (Proverbs 21:20). The Bible tells us to be savers, and God will bless our obedience in this area.

4. *Keep out of debt.* (See Romans 13:8.) In God's economy, the furniture is on the ceiling. Biblical principles are the opposite of the devil's schemes. Live on what you make. Trust God to meet your needs, instead of trusting loans. You'll find the Lord far more trustworthy to meet present and future needs than any loan you could trust for that purpose.

5. *Keep a budget.* (See 1 Corinthians 14:40.) A spending plan will help you keep control of your financial situation. You'll be prepared for the unusual. You'll plan to give, save, and spend. You'll be able to know how to adjust to the unexpected in both income

and spending needs.

6. *Work.* The Apostle Paul sums up the biblical principle of work as follows: "... Work heartily, as serving the Lord and not men" (Colossians 3:23 RSV).

Fortunately, as inflation increases, wages generally increase, too. However, many families today increase their spending more than their wages. With higher wages propelling them into higher tax brackets, they spend the wage increase without actually checking to see what's left to spend.

With spending often going for new cars or larger houses, the item purchased actually adds to future spending needs, reducing the amount available for basic necessities.

Inflation certainly is changing our lifestyles. Several years from now, we'll look back on today as the good old days. We'll remember when we drove large, air-conditioned cars wherever and whenever we wanted. We'll remember that most of us owned our own beautiful homes, comfort-conditioned year-round. We'll remember using cheap water to water our green grass, run garbage down our disposals, and take long, hot showers. We'll think fondly of our frequent travels, our charcoal-broiled steak,s and our frequent meals out.

I've never seen anyone beat inflation with debt. The people I see in the worst trouble financially are those who live beyond their means.

We must be ready to adjust our lifestyles. If the cost of air conditioning our houses goes so high we can't pay for it, we have some tough choices to make. One is to turn off the cooling system and suffer the heat. (The Bible, for example, has much to say about suffering, most of it relating to how much we can learn, grow, and depend on the Lord during our suffering.) Or we can cut out such things as travel, clothes, life insurance, college educations, recreation, and eating out. Borrowing money to pay for the air conditioning won't solve the problem. Getting angry at the utility company won't solve the problem. Demanding higher wages from our employers won't solve the problem. The inflation problem can be solved only when the elected representatives of our cities, states, and nation use the self control to say *no* to overspending and *yes* to living within our means. The inflation problem can be solved in your household when you say *no* to overspending and *yes* to living within your means.

Someone has said, "It is not the high cost of living that is our problem, but it is the cost of living high that is our problem."

Here are some practical things you can do to keep from being hit by rising costs:

1. *Turn off your air conditioner.* Rising utility costs will not affect you too much if you eliminate the costliest item.

2. *Stop eating out.* Our eating habits today allow for many more meals out than were normal a few years ago. Since service is a major factor in meals served in restaurants, the price of restaurant meals has increased more rapidly than dining at home.

3. *Make do with what you have.* Any item you don't buy keeps you from paying the inflated prices of the new item.

Making Do

Have you ever referred to those huge catalogues as "wish books?" *I wish* summarizes the state where most people live — the state of discontent.

The dictionary defines *discontent* as "a dislike of what one has and a desire for something different; feeling not satisfied; uneasiness; restlessness." As I ponder this definition, I think of so many people whose lives are characterized by discontent. They fill their bedrooms with king-size beds and their houses with everything imaginable. They then feel crowded, and they either build an addition onto their house or buy a bigger one. Meanwhile, the process of buying more "stuff" continues.

An unknown skeptic has summarized financial discontent in this way: "People buy things they don't need with money they don't have to impress neighbors they don't even like!" If you live now, or ever have lived, in a state of discontent, you know one word describes it all: *misery*. The cycle of wanting, shopping, buying, and filling doesn't add up. The total comes to an empty bank account plus an insatiable longing for still more stuff!

Shirley Rice, a Christian wife and mother, has had a great ministry in our home with her taped series and her booklet *The Christian Home, a Woman's View* (Norfolk, VA: The Tabernacle Church of Norfolk, 1965). In her chapter on "The Atmosphere of the Home," she gives feminine insights on women's attitudes toward "things":

> We haven't learned to "sit loose to the world and everything in it" as Matthew Henry says. "Whatever you have of the world in your hands, keep it out of your heart." We set great store by "things"; we are never satisfied with what we have. We push our husbands to get ahead; we covet this and that. Never being satisfied makes us tense. Proverbs 15:27 says "He that is greedy of gain troubleth his own house." David said in Psalms 131:2, "I have behaved myself as a weaned child" [KJV]. Are we weaned from our desires for things of a material nature? Covetousness begins when we cannot be content with what we have. It is not that you do not need a new rug, nor is it that it is wrong for you to have it; but the sin is that you cannot be content with what you have until such time as you can afford the new one.

The Bible clearly establishes God's principle of contentment: "Keep your life free from love of money, and be content with what you have; for he has said, 'I will never fail you nor forsake you' " (Hebrews 13:5 RSV).

You may already have noticed that contentment does not depend on what you have. Paul defines contented living, showing how our attitudes are the real key: "Our hearts ache, but at the same time we have the joy of the Lord. We are poor, but we give rich spiritual gifts to others. We own nothing, and yet we enjoy everything" (2 Corinthians 6:10).

Enjoyment and contentment do not depend on ownership. We would enjoy very little if ownership was the requirement.

I have had a pilot's license for many years. I can't imagine that anyone enjoys flying a small plane any more than I do. I've literally covered the United States by plane, exhilarated by the unique challenges of each trip. But I have never owned an airplane. For the amount of flying I do, it would cost me several thousand dollars more per year to own a plane instead of renting one.

Years ago, I calculated that my two daughters probably would choose to go to college. The dubious benefits of airplane ownership, when compared to the plan to have college funds set aside by the time of their high school graduation, motivated me to continue renting.

There were hassles in renting. I didn't always make every trip I planned. However, there were enough trips to log more than 100,000 miles. When time for college arrived, there was enough money set aside to pay the expenses.

The ownership of luxury items seldom makes sound financial sense. Campers, boats, cabins, and airplanes are all items that are costly to buy and maintain. Their upkeep also takes time — time that could be used for the Lord's work.

Bill Gothard, president of the Institute in Basic Youth Conflicts in Oak Brook, IL, defined *contentment* as "realizing that God has provided everything I need for my present circumstances." The man who is satisfied with little has everything. If you haven't got what you like, like what you have.

God revealed a very powerful principle to me early one morning while I was kneeling in prayer at our couch in the family room. The regular use of this prayer principle has the potential for eliminating discontent. The principle is that of *giving thanks* to God in prayer.

As I prayed, I was overwhelmed with thanksgiving to God for my wife and her spirit of contentment. I thanked Him that she was still content with the furniture in our family room. We had bought the couch from a neighbor many years earlier at a price of $50. Another couch, chair, and tables were hand-me-downs from Marjean's parents. We had refinished these things when the girls were babies. The breakfast table and chairs had been bought for $34 in a junk shop and had been antiqued.

I thought about all the men I knew whose wives were nagging them constantly for newer stuff. Then I thanked Him again for a contented wife. I remembered that my two daughters had been content to grow up with no color television set and had driven old cars. I thanked Him for Jenny and Amy's attitudes of contentment.

God's Word summarizes this principle in Psalm: "It is good to say, 'Thank you' to the Lord, to sing praises to the God who is above all gods. Every morning tell him, 'Thank you for your kindness,' and every evening rejoice in all his faithfulness" (Psalms 92:1, 2 TLB).

A simple jingle has helped us evaluate possible purchases in our home. You might measure all prospective purchases against its standards:

> *Use it up,*
> *Wear it out,*
> *Make it do,*
> *Do without.*

I once saw a sign that has kept me from many purchases: YOU HAVE NO IDEA OF THE THINGS YOU CAN DO WITHOUT —UNTIL YOU TRY. One January our family made a list of items we wanted to buy during the year. We agreed to not consider actually purchasing them until the middle of the year. In July, when we looked at the list, we were glad we hadn't bought some of the items; *we no longer wanted them*!

The world has some tremendous advertising tools that aim to create dissatisfaction in our lives. These devices are potent and very effective. Three powerful weapons of the advertising world bear examination so we can avoid their influence in our lives.

1. Television. One of my friends calls the TV set a "moron-o-scope." But those who create the commercials are far from morons. Their brainchildren are programmed to keep you from being content with what you have. Have you ever noticed that the half-hour of evening news, weather, and sports usually has 13 commercials, which make up one-fourth of the 30 minutes? Americans average many hours per day viewing television. During this time, scores of commercials are planned to motivate you to buy or to do something. Is it any wonder that contentment vanishes and wants increase in proportion to the amount of TV viewing time?

To bring the TV set into focus as an influential factor, I recall one study that indicated between the key developmental ages of 3 and 18, the average American is spending 22,000 hours watching television. The same American, if he/she is a better-than-average church goer, will spend at the most 3,000 hours in church and Sunday school.

Which influence will have the greater impact?

Marjean and I know a Hesston, KS, family who never owned a television set. The six children grew up without the benefit of this modern electronic wonder. If you shared the hospitality of their home, as we have been privileged to do on many occasions, you would be thrilled with the courtesy, the family spirit, and the contentment that were apparent. Obviously, there's been more involved than the absence of a television set. But they have taken their stand; they are a family of participants — in music, sports, and family duties — instead of a household of spectators.

2. *Shopping*. A Wichita physician and his wife once devised a very interesting experiment for grocery shopping. The wife ordered all their groceries over the phone at one of a handful of stores which would deliver groceries to their home. When she ordered by phone, she had to work from a list. It helped control the grocery bill when she wasn't exposed to the techniques of the hidden persuaders who lay out and develop our supermarkets in such a way as to encourage us to buy more than we need. Although the prices were higher where she phoned, the couple figured they could afford to pay more on the items ordered compared to impulse purchases made while shopping in person.

Most of us have learned that the more shopping we do, the more we spend. My wife proved this when she went on several shopping trips with our oldest daughter Jenny, prior to Jenny's leaving for college. For the first time in many months, I found Marjean's wants increasing beyond her clothing budget. Out in stores she found "bargains" and "cute things" she felt she could not live without. Fortunately, the reality of a budget kept her from overspending.

Marjean also has learned not to send me by the store on my way home from work. Hungry husbands make poor shoppers.

When we were expecting our first child, a door-to-door saleswoman appeared with an offer for a long-term subscription to a magazine and a large, "free" medical book. Marjean promptly signed on the dotted line and wrote out her check, feeling pleased with herself.

A few minutes later she began to think about how she would explain the "good deal" to me. Was it really a deal? Would I be angry? Had she paid too much?

She wanted to back out. She raced out the door and found the saleswoman up at the end of the block.

Would you believe the woman said she already had put the order in the mailbox?

When I came home from work, Marjean told me the story. She had subscribed to the magazine for several years. Even then, the price per issue was above the newsstand price. A quick check of a common mail-order catalogue showed reduced prices per issue for shorter-term subscriptions. Our so-called free medical book was not free at all.

3. Newspapers, magazines, and catalogues. Advertising is calculated to get you, the reader, to buy. Spending time looking at ads is an excellent way to lose your contentment with what you have.

Some weary victims have gone so far as to cancel their magazine subscriptions and ask that their names be removed from catalogue lists. Within the last 30 days, I have received 25 catalogues containing more than 1,200 pages of colorful, tempting merchandise.

Avoiding these enticements of television, shopping, magazines, and catalogues can be a great aid in controlling your contentment. God didn't command us to be content so He could make us miserable; sowing discontent is what reaps misery.

The fruit of contentment is abundant. Joy, peace, and a thankful spirit are three of these fruits.

One of Paul's most exciting passages — and certainly one of his most challenging — is in Philippians: "Not that I was ever in need, for I have learned how to get along happily whether I have much or little. I know how to live on almost nothing or with everything. I have learned the secret of contentment in every situation, whether it be a full stomach or hunger, plenty or want" (Philippians 4:11, 12 TLB).

Note that this is followed in verse 13 by Paul confidently saying, "... I can do everything God asks me to with the help of Christ who gives me the strength and power."

God is the secret of contentment!

The Inflation Mentality

"Buy now! If you don't, the price will be so high later that you may never be able to afford it."

Such a philosophy was expressed in a poem I heard in college. The theme was marriage, but the subject could be anything else you want now but don't have the money to buy:

The bride bent over with age, leaned over her cane
Her steps uncertain need guiding. . . .
While down the church aisle with a wan, toothless smile,
The groom in a wheel chair gliding.

And who is this elderly couple thus wed?
You'll find when you've closely explored it,
That this is that rare, most conservative pair
Who WAITED 'TIL THEY COULD AFFORD IT!

In recent years, not many customers waited 'til they could afford it.

But why wait? Won't whatever you buy cost more in the future? Isn't it smart planning to buy now at a lower price and pay back later with the dollars made cheaper by inflation?

Two illustrations from my counseling may reveal two opposite approaches to the inflation problem. A couple came to me with debts beyond their current ability to pay. When they'd bought their house one year earlier, they'd had no debt. Now they owed $2,400. What had happened?

The house they'd bought to save money had cost more than they had planned. Insurance, taxes, and maintenance were all items to which they had closed their eyes when they'd bought their home. Each month they sank deeper into debt.

Solomon described their situation and the reason for their plight: "For you closed your eyes to the facts and did not choose to reverence and trust the Lord. . . . That is why you must eat the bitter fruit of having your own way and experience the full terrors of the pathway you have chosen" (Proverbs 1:29, 31 TLB). Can you imagine the trauma they faced as they attempted to reduce spending by the $200 a month they had been overspending — and then by *another* $200 a month, to repay the debt?

Investing to Save

It makes no sense to buy something now if the expenses it will add to your budget will cause you to overspend your income. But it does make sense to buy something now if it will lower your expenses now and in the future — if, that is, you can afford the purchase!

Some time ago, an insulation salesman called on me. With my permission, he showed me that the insulation in my attic was lacking the recommended R value. By adding R-19 to my ceiling insulation, he estimated 20 percent of my gas and electric bills would be saved. He quoted the price of $675 to insulate my attic.

Remembering what Solomon declared — "Only a simpleton believes what he is told! A prudent man checks to see where he is going" (Proverbs 14:15 TLB) — I decided to gather more facts. A check with the city energy department confirmed that R-30 was the recommended amount of insulation in my house; its estimate of utility savings was for 10 percent instead of 20.

Noting another Proverb — "Plans go wrong with too few counselors; many counselors bring success" (Proverbs 15:22 TLB) — I sought more counsel. The specialist at the local electric company said experience with its customers proved 10-percent electric and gas savings was possible.

Offsetting the $675 cost of insulation, I calculated the cumulative savings, over a period of years, at 10 percent of my utility cost (assuming utilities increased no more than 10 percent per year). I found that within six years, my savings in reduced utility bills should cover the $675 I would have invested in the insulation.

That seemed like a sensible investment that would reap dollar returns to me as long as I lived in that house.

In the first illustration, the couple increased their monthly expenses beyond their capacity. The insulation example was an investment that was projected to lower expenses.

Which would appear to you to be the prudent investment?
Which alternative looks like the best way to beat inflation?

Marjean's 2¢: Investing or Spending?

I often hear someone say, "I invested in a new iron" or a
new set of dishes or similar items. Inwardly I smile because of
the use of the term "invest."

Webster's definition of invest is "to use (money) to buy
something that is expected to produce a profit, or income, or
both." I wonder if that person really does intend for that iron or
set of dishes to produce a profit or income. Or is he using that
word to justify his spending the money? Perhaps he's even
buying it on time.

We all need to be careful not to fool ourselves into thinking
we are *investing* money when we are really *spending* it.

5: Preparing For the Car Squeeze

The automobile is one item that keeps many families in a financial pinch. How easy it is to become discontented with your present car and succumb to the fever to trade for a newer model. New car fever can't be cured with aspirin, but it may be cooled by looking at some cold, hard facts about car costs.

Automobiles are seldom worn out when they are traded for later models. The proof of this is the fact that someone will buy your trade-in (probably for several hundred dollars more than you received for it), expecting to drive it many thousands of miles.

Are You Sure You Need to Trade?

Consider the reasons usually given for trading in a car: age, mileage, and needed repairs.

AGE is no reason to trade in a car. I remember my mother's car being some 20 years old. Having spent most all of its nondriving time in a garage, the condition of its body was better than that of most cars half its age. While some cars are old after one year, a car can be relatively new after several years, if it has had excellent care.

I once served communion monthly to a couple who were 85 and 86 years old. When I arrived one Sunday the woman was out in the garage. There I saw the car they had bought in 1940 — a 1940 Master Deluxe Chevrolet. In the 36 years they'd had the car, it had been driven a total of 57,000 miles, and the engine had never had any major repairs. The car still provided useful transportation for these folks.

That the car was still powerful was proven when the lady, attempting to back the car out of the garage, unintentionally put it in

low gear instead of reverse. The car shot straight forward, removing
the back of the garage in one big piece. Not one dent or scratch was
on the front of the car, even though the entire back of the garage had
been moved about 10 feet into the back yard.

When the couple would drive the car, they found people oohing
and aahing over it. They even had people follow them home and ask
them about buying the car.

Should these people have been advised to trade for a newer
model just because their car was 36 years old?

MILEAGE usually is insufficient justification to trade cars.
The chairman of our deacons is a mechanic. He tells me that with
proper maintenance and repairs, most cars can be expected to
perform satisfactorily up to 150,000 miles or more.

A survey I made at one automobile dealership revealed that
during a three-month period, the average number of miles on the cars
that were traded in was 60,285. Of a substantial number of cars, only
four had mileage in excess of 100,000; the highest mileage on any
trade-in was 112,112. That's hardly driving your car to a successful
conclusion.

These facts support the proposition that most people trade in
when their cars still have more than half of their useful lives
remaining.

REPAIRS. Buying a new car because your present car needs
repairs seems almost as absurd as committing suicide because you
need surgery.

A youth director was sent to me by her father for counsel about
her car. Her present vehicle had less than 100,000 miles on it and was
less than 10 years old, but was suddenly in need of $200 worth of
repairs. Her father thought she should not waste any more money
repairing the old clunker but should buy a new one.

As we studied the facts of the two alternatives, we clearly saw
that the economics favored fixing the car she had.

Compare such costs as taxes, insurance, and depreciation — not
to mention the price of a new car and the cost of financing. In most
cases, it costs more to own and operate a newer car than an older one.

Find the Facts

Solomon, in the Book of Proverbs, contrasts the wise man with the fool. When it comes to facts, he says, "The wise man looks ahead. The fool attempts to fool himself and won't face facts" (Proverbs 14:8 TLB). You'd be surprised how many people are fools when it comes to cars. I easily spot people fooling themselves, when they show me their budgets.

Sam was a business executive earning more than $36,000 annually. During the past year, since he had moved into his present house, he had accumulated more than $6,000 in short-term debts. The budget he and his wife sent me showed spending equal to income. Obviously, you don't go $500 a month in the hole unless you are spending more than you make. Sam's budget evidently had some leaks.

Since the investigative techniques of Sherlock Holmes long have been favorites of mine, I was challenged to look for the leaks. Much financial counseling has taught me that the one place to begin is to examine closely the car category of the budget.

Sam's monthly budget figures showed the following under transportation:

Gas	$160
Repairs	30
Insurance	50
Total	$240

My next step was to follow Solomon's advice: "Get the facts at any price, and hold on tightly to all the good sense you can get." (Proverbs 23:23 TLB).

I called Sam. "How many cars do you have, Sam?"

"Three," he replied.

"How many miles a month are you driving your cars?" I inquired. (Since his last move was to a house 22 miles from his work, five miles from his teen-agers' school, and two miles from shopping,

I suspected his family was driving many miles.)

After a quick look at his odometers, Sam was back on the phone. "Three thousand," he said. "But that sounds too high to me."

"Not surprising," I replied. "That's about 1,400 miles for your car and 800 miles apiece for each of your other cars. Three thousand miles a month sounds right to me for your active family."

Next I took out my calculator and divided the $240 his budget showed for car expenses by the 3,000 miles they were driving, and arrived at $.08 per mile.

"Can you drive your car for eight cents a mile, Sam?"

"No way," he answered.

Here was one huge hole in Sam's budget. Assuming a conservative $.25 per mile to drive his cars, Sam's spending plan was short by a whopping $510 a month ($.25 minus $.08 equals $.17, times 3,000 miles equals $510).

Now are *you* ready for these facts? At $.25 per mile, Sam's family actually was spending $750 each month to drive their cars — not the $240 they were budgeting.

How about you? Do you have a gaping hole in your budget dike because you are trying to fool yourself on what it costs to drive *your* car?

Most people calculate the cost of gas and insurance and an occasional emergency repair as the cost of driving their car. When I show them the "Gas Tank Facts" (see table, next page), they look at me as if I'm trying to exaggerate the figures or put something over on them. How do you feel about these gas tank facts?

Every time you fill your tank with gas — the dollar amount shown in the left column — you have just as surely spent the amount in the right-hand column during the time you burned the gas. When you put $12 of gas in your tank, did you also put aside $40.45 for those other certain expenses? If not, you will be surprised when they crop up as a budget buster later.

At one seminar, a woman with an unbelieving look on her face raised her hand. "What are those 'certain future expenses?' " she asked. I answered, "Insurance, taxes, repairs, maintenance, and money to replace this car when you change cars." The unbelieving look continued. She simply said, "Oh." She was too polite to say, "I don't believe it. It doesn't cost me that much to drive my car. Unless you prove it to me, I just won't believe it, Mr. Fooshee."

She was right. The costs of car ownership are so unbelievable that I need to prove them to myself again and again. So fasten your seat belt and hang on.

Gas Tank Facts

Gas cost	Did I save for certain future expenses?*
$ 5.00	$16.83
6.00	20.22
7.00	23.63
8.00	27.03
9.00	30.43
10.00	33.83
11.00	37.23
12.00	40.45
13.00	43.86
14.00	47.26
15.00	50.66
16.00	54.06
17.00	57.46
18.00	60.86

* Includes insurance, taxes, maintenance, repairs, and car replacement for a new car driven 10 years at an average of 10,000 miles a year.

To illustrate your actual driving expenses, assume you spend $12 for 10 gallons of gas at $1.20 per gallon. Add $40.45 for those "certain future expenses" indicated in the right-hand column (total: $50.45). If your car gets, let's say, 20 miles to a gallon of gas, you'll drive 200 miles on that 10 gallons purchased. Dividing your cost ($50.45) by 200 miles, you'll find that you're paying $.252 per mile to drive your car.

While you may be getting better than 20 miles to the gallon, never overlook those "certain future expenses. . . ."

Seeing Is Believing

"Twenty-five cents a mile! Absurd. I know we don't spend anywhere near 25 cents a mile to drive our cars!" With such unbelief, dozens of counselees have returned from our financial sessions blindly ignoring true car costs. They continue to fool themselves into believing they can afford two cars, long weekend trips, cars for their kids, and other luxuries.

Jesus said to the disciples, "Do you have eyes but fail to see, and ears but fail to hear. . . ?" (Mark 8:18 NIV). My goal is to show you so clearly what it costs to drive a car that you'll literally hear the meter ticking every time you make a decision about your car.

Let's make some assumptions:

Car cost	$11,000
Miles driven a year	12,000
Number of years driven	5
Car value when sold	$1,600
Gas mileage average	20 MPG
Drivers	2 adults

CAR COST

Starting with a car costing $11,000 and assuming you will replace it with an $11,000 car five years from now, you will need to save $9,400. Here's the breakdown:

Cost of present car	$11,000
Sell car in five years	1,600
Cost to replace present car	9,400

$9,400 divided by 5 years = $1,880 per year or $156.66 per month
$9,400 divided by 60,000 miles = .156¢ per mile
You will need to set aside $156.66 each month, or $.156 each

mile you drive, to have enough money to replace your car five years from now, or 60,000 miles later.

GAS COST

Feeding gas to your 20 MPG guzzler over 12,000 miles means you must buy 600 gallons of gas. At an average price of $1.20 per gallon, you've spent $720.

In case you're driving a real gas miser, you might be doing better:

12,000 miles at	Gallons	Total cost at $1.20/gallon	Cost per mile
20 MPG	600	$720	$.06
25 MPG	480	576	.048
30 MPG	400	480	.04
40 MPG	300	360	.03

INSURANCE

Insurance rates vary infinitely and are based on the city, state, company, drivers, car use, make and model, and coverage.

Let's assume you can obtain insurance for $636 a year. For that car, insurance totals $.053 a mile for your 12,000 annual miles.

INTEREST COST

Since the vast majority of all cars are purchased with borrowed money, we need to include an interest amount. Most people use their old car plus a little cash for the down payment. We'll assume $10,000 will be financed at 10 percent for three years. Interest totals $3,000 and adds $.05 per mile over the first 36,000 miles.

TAXES & LICENSES

Taxes also vary widely from location to location. We'll assume you're being taxed both a state personal property tax and an annual license on your used car, and those two figures total approximately $600 for the five years you drive the car. That's another $.01 a mile.

REPAIRS & MAINTENANCE

Beware! This category is the trouble spot. People seem to think car repairs are: unusual, emergencies, and bad luck. Not so! They are: common, usual, routine, and necessary.

Add up the annual cost of a couple of radial tires, a battery, five oil changes, two new shocks, a brake job, hose replacements, a minor tune-up, a service call to jumpstart the car or change a tire, a wheel alignment (or balancing and tire rotation), a new water pump or fuel pump. . . .

You may think, "This is absurd. I won't need all those things in any one year."

You may be right. But remember, we've *left out* some other things that might add to your costs, such as:

Vandalism
Accident
Electrical repair
Muffler & tail pipe
Carburetor overhaul
Air conditioner repair
Heater repair
2 more radials
Alternator
Starter
Transmission replacement
Valve job

Take your pick. Repairs and service easily can total thousands of dollars per year. If you get by for less than that this year, just wait 'til next year.

The only way I came to believe these figures myself was to keep a small repair-and-maintenance log book in my glove compartment. That black book made a believer of me. Why don't you try it?

We'll estimate repair costs conservatively: 6 cents per mile.

SUMMARY

Here are some typical costs for our $11,000 car.

Total cost	Per mile
Car cost	$.156
Gas	.060
Insurance	.053
Interest	.050
Taxes & licenses	.010
Repairs & maintenance	.060
Total	$.389

The Ticking Meter

Our hypothetical car is costing us almost $.40 each mile. Yours may be costing less, or it may be costing more.

If you are driving a car that costs less than our $11,000 one, your car cost is less. If you average more than 20 MPG, your gas cost is less. If you live where insurance rates are lower than those used, you'll save a little on insurance. If you buy for cash instead of financing, you have no interest cost (but you do lose the interest you would have earned if the cash had been invested in savings instead of spent on a car). If you have a car that seldom needs repairs, or if you perform all your own repairs, you'll save some more here.

My experience is that most families don't buy used cars, do pay more than $11,000 for new cars, do borrow money to pay for them, do drive more than 12,000 miles a year, do have terrific repair bills, and would drool at the low insurance costs I've quoted. And to make the car costs really exciting, they are driving two or more cars, often with teen-age drivers who send the insurance, mileage, and repairs to even higher levels.

Are you willing to settle for $.40 a mile?

Seeing is believing! Buy your cars with your eyes wide open to the real costs. Calculate your own costs of your next car. Then put those costs in your budget. If they fit well, rejoice. If they blow the budget, consider an alternative.

Marjean's 2¢: "These Figures Boggle My Mind!"

As a housewife, my question is: "How can I help ease the pressure of continually mounting transportation costs?"

First of all, I can be content with the car I have. My 15-year-old car gets me every place I need to go. We keep it up by checking the oil, battery, hoses, and radiator water regularly.

Speaking of "places I need to go," that is the second way I can help cut the costs. My week is planned so that errands and grocery shopping can be limited to one or two days a week. I know when and where I will be on certain days of the week. So such things as dropping off or picking up the cleaning can be done on my way some place else, instead of making a special trip out for that. I resist, like the plague, the pull to jump in my car to run one errand for a special need.

When the girls were at home with lessons, Girl Scouts, and other activities, I planned my errands around their trips. Encourage your family to help with this. Post an "I need" list on the refrigerator. When anyone runs out of an item, jot it down there. Ultimately incorporate it into your shopping list.

Inform your family of the day you will be out running errands. Then any of their needs can be taken care of at that time. As you "do nothing from selfishness or conceit, but in humility," you "look not only to [your] . . . own interests, but also to the interests of others" (Philippians 2:3,4 RSV). You are working together in a family.

6: The House Squeeze: It's Outasight

At lunch one day, Jerry, a young attorney, asked, "How much should I save before I can buy a house?"

"That's a good question," I replied.

After thinking about it for a minute, I said, "About $14,000. That will give you a $8,000 down payment on an $80,000 house, $3,000 closing and moving costs, and $3,000 left over for emergencies."

I soon discovered that was a bad answer.

Look what could have happened to Jerry if he'd taken my off-the-cuff answer seriously:

House cost	$80,000
Down payment	8,000
Mortgage (30 years at 8%)	$72,000

	Monthly	Annually
Mortgage payment	$ 525.60	$6,307
Insurance (.5% of the cost)	33.33	400
Taxes (2.5% of the cost)	166.66	2,000
Maintenance (2% of the cost)	133.33	1,600
Utilities (4% of the cost)	266.66	3,200
Totals	$1,125.58	$13,507

Jerry's projected gross income is $30,000, or $2,500 monthly.

Here's what the shelter expenses look like, compared to his income:

| Monthly expense | $1,126 | Annual expense | $13,507 |
| Monthly income | $2,500 | Annual income | $30,000 |

His shelter would be taking 45 percent of his gross income. *You* try balancing your budget after paying out 45 percent of all your gross income for the place where you live. If you succeed, write me and let me know how you did it.

Realtors used to tell people they could buy a house that cost two-and-one-half times their annual gross income. Recently I've read articles suggesting your monthly house payment can total 25 percent of your gross income.

My own rule of thumb is that you may afford a house not to exceed 1.7 times your annual gross family income.

If you buy a house costing this amount:	Your annual gross earnings will need to be at least:
$30,000	$ 17,647
35,000	20,588
40,000	23,529
45,000	26,470
50,000	29,411
55,000	32,352
60,000	35,294
70,000	41,176
80,000	47,059
90,000	52,941
100,000	58,823
120,000	70,588
140,000	82,352
160,000	94,117
200,000	117,647

Outasight!

Such figures are so far "outasight" that large numbers of people are refusing to believe them. Instead, they listen to the realtors' smooth pitch to "bite the bullet." "You'll never be able to buy this cheaply again," they say. And they "bite the bullet." They reason that the payment is just a few dollars more than their present payment. And it will be a super investment. And they will cut some place else.

Most families I've counseled have increased their family debt by $150 to 500 a month from the time they bought their house to the time they sought help for their financial problems.

Outasight!

That's right! Outasight because they didn't look to see what was involved beyond that monthly house payment.

Marjean's 2¢: The House That's "Just Perfect"

"But this house is just perfect for us!" This is the cry we hear when George shows the couple the facts about the figures on the house they want to buy. (If they haven't already bought it!)

I shudder when I remember the house I thought was "just perfect" for us. We had been engaging in the Sunday afternoon sport of touring open houses for sale. There was a house not far from ours — same school district, grocery stores, and friends. We loved it. Oh, there were a few minor problems with it, but we could overlook them.

The asking price was more than George was willing to pay, but he made an offer. In the time that lapsed before we heard from the owner, I had mentally moved into the house, arranged our furniture in each of the rooms, decided which bedrooms would be occupied by whom, and entertained our first guests. Would you believe that when the owner turned down our offer, George refused to go up? I was crushed. After all, it was "just perfect" for us.

How thankful I am now that George got the facts and stuck to them, despite my pleas, and that we waited on God's house, which truly is "just perfect" for us.

The Shocking Truth

Let's suppose Jerry opts for a $60,000 house. Let's look at the figures and hear them speak. My friend's income of $30,000 a year means he will have to struggle to pay for a $60,000 house and balance his budget at the same time. Here's the way I wrote out the estimates for him:

House cost $60,000
Down payment   -6,000
Mortgage (30 years at 8%) $54,000

	Monthly	Annually
Mortgage payment	$394.20	$4,730
Insurance (.5% of the cost)	25.00	300
Taxes (2.5% of the cost)	125.00	1,500
Maintenance (2% of the cost)	100.00	1,200
Utilities (4% of the cost)	200.00	2,400
Totals	$844.20	$10,130

Let's assume all expenses for the place where you live must not exceed 30 percent of your total gross income. Thirty percent of Jerry's $30,000 income is $9,000. His housing costs will exceed the maximum allowable by $1,130 annually.

His alternatives are: Buy a $50,000 house with a $5,000 down payment; annual expenses on the same formula total $8,442, slightly below the $9,000 rule of thumb. Or if he paid $4,000 more down, bringing his down payment to $10,000, his mortgage on the $60,000 house would be reduced to $50,000, which would lower his monthly payment significantly. His total annual cost would be $9,780, closer to his $9,000 maximum.

The assumption in each of these exercises is that you make only a 10-percent down payment. In reality, depending on the circumstances and the current housing market, you may be required to pay more.

On the following page are the figures for two houses with expenses worked out to show you what you might need in order to operate some higher-priced homes.

House cost	$100,000
Down payment	10,000
Mortgage (30 years at 8%)	$90,000

	Monthly	Annually
Mortgage payment	$657.00	$7,884
Insurance (.5% of the cost)	41.66	500
Taxes (2.5% of the cost)	208.33	2,500
Maintenance (2% of the cost)	166.66	2,000
Utilities (4% of the cost)	333.33	4,000
Totals	$1,406.98	$16,884

The gross income necessary to support this house, according to my rule of thumb stated earlier, is $58,823 per year, or about $4,902 monthly.

House cost	$120,000
Down payment	-12,000
Mortgage (30 years at 8%)	$108,000

	Monthly	Annually
Mortgage payment	$ 788.40	$ 9,460
Insurance (.5% of the cost)	50.00	600
Taxes (2.5% of the cost)	250.00	3,000
Maintenance (2% of the cost)	200.00	2,400
Utilities (4% of the cost)	400.00	4,800
Totals	$1,688.40	$20,260

The gross income necessary to support this house is $70,588 per year, or $5,882 monthly.

One young man said to me, "I thought shelter expense meant only the house payment." A young lady was proudly showing pictures of their new home to a friend. She said, "In a few months we'll find out if we can afford it."

Rules of thumb are just that; your own figures may check out higher or lower. But *get the facts*! After you've moved into your new home is too late to find out you can't afford it.

Use this guide to figure your own potential housing costs. Past experience on taxes and utilities will be available from the listing. Your agent will quote you on the insurance. Maintenance at two percent is a good estimate.

Cost of house	_____
Less down payment	_____
Mortgage	_____

	Monthly	Annually
Monthly payment	_____	_____
Insurance	_____	_____
Taxes	_____	_____
Maintenance	_____	_____
Utilities	_____	_____
Total	_____	_____

Use the monthly payment schedule for mortgage interest amounts from the following:

Monthly payment for 30 years at:	Per $1,000 of mortgage
8.00%	$7.30
9.00%	8.05
10.00%	8.78
11.00%	9.53

Some comments will be helpful on the expense estimates. Insurance on your home will depend on many factors. Location, type of construction, age of house, size of house, types of coverage, deductibles — each will affect what you pay. The best way is to get estimates from two or three insurance agents. Taxes also vary according to city, state, rates, referendum directives, and a host of other factors. Maintenance—maintenance—maintenance: Doesn't it sound absurd to budget two percent of the cost of your home for annual maintenance? If you own your own home now, go back and look at your check stubs for four years. If your house has averaged $70,000 in market value, at two percent of the value of your house each year, you would have spent $5,600 in four years for maintenance.

Here are some of the items that aren't included in the house payment, insurance, tax, or utility categories, which you may have to count on in the maintenance category:

Repairs on:	Purchase of or replacement of:
Furnace	Furnace
Air conditioner	Air conditioner
Plumbing	Water tank
Sewers	Wiring

Lights & wiring
Oven
Burners
Disposal
Refrigerator
Freezer
Doors
Windows
Washer
Dryer
Small appliances
Dishwasher
Sidewalks
Driveways
Siding
Roof
Water softener
Cleaning, painting, or
    maintenance inside
    & outside house
Carpets
Floors
Insect or termite control
Insulation

Oven
Disposal
Refrigerator
Freezer
Washer
Dryer
Water softener
Small appliances
Dishwasher
Dishes
Linens
Mattresses
Furniture
Carpet
Floor coverings
Roof
Trees
Shrubs & flowers
Sidewalks
Driveways
Fences

In addition to those, you have outside expenses:

Yard care
Fertilizer
Mowing
Spraying

Edging
Snow removal
Tree care

Your list may not include all the things on my list. Great! Scratch them off. However, you may have special items that aren't on my list.

A homeowner faces constant surprises. One day I heard what sounded like running water coming from my basement. Investigation proved my water tank had sprung a leak. Solutions: Use cold water or buy a new tank.

My roof was shot. Alternatives: Leaks in my house or buy a new roof. Major repairs of this nature can run to five figures.

The shocking truth: It costs money to own your own home!

Marjean's 2¢: The Shocking Truth

That list of possible repairs or replacements is shocking! What if they all need repair at once? You can't plan for that in your maintenance, can you? No, but you can learn to wait on some repairs, until you can plan for them.

"But how can I wait, when my dishwasher has broken down?" Just as some friends of ours did. They enlisted the family troops and had a good talk time while washing and drying dishes. The same family's garbage disposal broke down. They found they could carry garbage to the trash. Then the ultimate: No family of six can do without a washing machine — but they did, when theirs went on the blink. They lacked the cash to repair or replace all those items at once, so they went to the laundromat. My friend reported that at least two of the family members went to the laundry each time, and they had some great conversations. For "we know that in everything God works for good with those who love him, who are called according to his purpose" (Romans 8:28 RSV). His purpose is for us to trust Him and wait, instead of plunging ahead to spend money we do not have.

7: Some Thoughts
On the Working Mother

Tight family finances frequently trigger the decision for a wife to go to work. For most single mothers, it's virtually a necessity.

Why do mothers work? How do they fare financially?

Will you assume with me that one good reason most mothers work is for the money? Few ever tell me they really *want* to go to work if they have small children. Since so many mothers with small children work outside the home, the financial benefits must be tremendous.

But they aren't! Especially for the working wife and mother.

In many professions, women still earn less than men. I have even seen cases in which the costs of the mother's working exceeded her income.

The Bottom Line for the Working Mother

What is the potential net income of a working wife and mother? We'll give two examples, both of which assume her husband is making $36,000 a year, there are two children involved, the family tithes its gross income, and the woman is not a professional in a high-income bracket. The figures are shown in the chart on the next page.

Remember that when you work, federal, state, and Social Security taxes will claim a fourth to a third of your nondeductible income. The more you earn, the greater percentage you'll pay in taxes.

66

	Example 1	Example 2	Fill in yours
Wife's gross income/year	$12,168.00	$18,304.00	_____
Wife's gross income/week	234.00	352.00	_____
Weekly expenses:			
Tithe	23.40	35.20	_____
Taxes/Social Security	59.00	96.00	_____
Transportation	10.00	10.00	_____
(10 trips of 4 miles @ .25 a mile)			
Lunch & coffee breaks	18.00	18.00	_____
Restaurants & carry-outs	24.00	24.00	_____
Extra clothes	0.00	20.00	_____
Beauty shop	18.00	18.00	_____
Other bought-it-with-my-money expenses	20.00	20.00	_____
Daycare	60.00	60.00	_____
(1 child preschool)			
Subtract expenses	$252.40	$299.20	_____
Net addition to family income	-18.40	+50.80	_____

Those Pesky Little Extra Expenses

Assuming a commitment to pay God and Caesar, the tax and tithe amounts are not open to debate. Let's examine the other expense categories:

TRANSPORTATION. The assumption is that the working mother will drive 40 more miles each week going to and from daycare and to and from work than if she were not working. Assuming she's driving an older car that is paid for, she's spending 25¢ a mile (for gas, oil, and repairs, with some set aside to replace the car she's driving), for an additional weekly expense of $10.

Her weekly driving totals 172 more miles a month than if she were not working. Your records may show that the working mother drives less when she is working, because she doesn't have all day to shop, take the children on visits, or drive other places. My own observation is that working mothers often use their cars to shop during lunch hours. They also do more driving in the evenings and on Saturdays, taking the children out.

Marjean never worked outside the home. Careful records revealed that her total driving during our children's preteen years never exceeded 4,000 miles a year (77 miles weekly). Expert planning enabled her to do all her shopping, church work, doctor visits, children's parties, lessons, and school functions within the 4,000 miles a year. With both teenagers driving, the total jumped to 9,700 miles during those high school years.

Keep mileage records. You'll soon know whether your working adds to your miles driven.

LUNCHES AND COFFEE BREAKS. Most working mothers have little time for lunch preparation from refrigerator left-overs. Also, coffee, soft drinks, and snacks during coffee breaks easily can add 50¢ to several dollars a day to expenses. The sky's the limit on purchased lunches, but counting tips and taxes, you reasonably might spend $3 for a bowl of soup or a small salad and iced tea. The $3 daily lunch, plus an average of 60¢ a day for snacks, totals $18 weekly.

You may spend more or less. Again, some record keeping will provide the key to your real expenses.

RESTAURANTS AND CARRY-OUTS. Show me a working mother who doesn't take her family out to eat more than the nonworking mother, and I'll show you a rare woman.

The amazing growth of the fast-food industry should be proof enough that a notable percentage of all food dollars are spent eating meals away from home. Wendy's, McDonald's, Hardee's, Burger King, Pizza Hut, and/or other chains occupy prominent locations in almost any American town. They are in business because we are eating out more than ever before.

The more the mother makes, the more likely she is to spend for the "treats" out. A family of four easily can spend $15 for a meal at a chain burger restaurant, more at fish or pizza chains — perhaps double for Sunday lunch at a cafeteria.

Assuming three meals a day, a family of four requires 84 meals a week. If the working mother and father eat out or send out for lunch, the children buy lunch at school, and the family visit a chain restaurant twice a week, they're buying and eating a third of their meals away from home. That's not at all uncommon in America today. Even if you don't eat out this often, consider that each time you *do* eat out, you're probably spending substantially more than you would spend for a meal prepared at home.

Be honest. Because you work, do you and your family eat more meals out?

EXTRA CLOTHES. Most working mothers find that their wardrobes need to be larger for work than for full-time homemaking. The pressure from coworkers who show up each season in new styles takes its toll. The wear and tear on clothing worn all day, at regular intervals, is a factor. The need for a nicer coat to replace the one you've made do — which looks more shabby, since you wear it daily in all kinds of weather — will provoke you to buy a new coat.

An extra $20 a week will allow for new purchases and dry-cleaning. Depending on the quality of dresses, coats, blouses, pantsuits, sweaters, slacks, coats, raincoats, shoes, lingerie, and gloves you buy, your expenses may be more or less than our example.

My own experience is that working mothers feel they're justified in dressing a "little nicer." And the more they earn, the more they spend.

BEAUTY SHOP. A working mother has precious little time to care for herself or sit peacefully in a quiet place. Most feel the beauty shop routine helps their spirits and their looks. As I head to town shortly after 6 A.M, I'm always surprised to see open beauty shops.

They open early to serve working women.

The cost? Let's say $25 for a shampoo and set and cut. You'd need to add $45 for a periodic permanent, $15 to 30 for an occasional manicure. And don't forget to count the stuff you buy that sits in sight while your hair is drying. Such displays are not accidents; people often buy what is close at hand.

You may or may not have this expense.

BOUGHT-IT-WITH-MY-OWN-MONEY EXPENSES. You are earning $12 to 18,000 a year, or even more. Why not a little splurge now and then for the family? For example:

- Extra clothes for the children.
- More expensive Christmas gifts.
- A skiing vacation at spring break.
- Something really nice that your husband's always wanted but could never afford.
- A special meal out with your husband at a really nice restaurant.

My experience in this area is that $20 a week for such items would prove to be conservative, in the course of a full year.

DAYCARE. The going rate in Wichita, KS, for preschoolers now is $60 to 90 per child, per week. For school-age children who need latchkey care in the early morning and/or after school, the weekly cost is $35. What are your child care costs?

Is It Worth It?

Some women maintain that they don't eat out or carry out food just because they are working. Others don't go to the beauty shop. On the other hand, we haven't included those pesky "office collections," birthday and shower and special occasion gifts for coworkers, and other common workplace expenses. Nor have we allowed for decreased income from days not worked because of sick children or emergencies at home.

Total all your extra expenses that are connected with your work. Subtract those expenses from your earnings, and you have what is called "the bottom line:" your profit from your work, the amount you keep as a result of all the hours you are away from children and home in order to work.

What is your net? Now divide it by the 50 hours a week you are away from home, driving to and from work, working and lunch times, and you see your hourly net income. Take a good, long, hard look at it.

Is it worth the cost? Your cost includes the taxes and expenses. Your cost is having someone else spend those fleeting hours with your children. Your cost is being a part-time helper to your husband. Your cost is busy, busy, busy. What do you think?

Does a wife/mother's earnings from a full-time job enable her to measure up to the wife described in Proverbs? "If you can find a truly good wife, she is worth more than precious gems!" (Proverbs 31:10 TLB). Her net income, as analyzed above, may hardly sound like precious gems.

Some other characteristics of the godly woman described in Proverbs 31 include such activities as these:

- Richly satisfying her husband's needs.
- Helping her husband.
- Preparing breakfast for her household.
- Watching for bargains.
- Sewing for her family.
- Sewing for the poor.

How could a wife away from home 50 hours a week be expected to fulfill such responsibilities? How can a mother supplement the family income and still have time to manage the home?

Ways to save money at home by a wife "working" as a comparative shopper, a creative cook with planned menus, and a seamstress doing simple alterations and clothing repairs are practically unlimited.

Consider two married mothers:

Harried Harriet arrives home exhausted from the hassles

of the office and hastily whips up a late dinner before cleaning up the house, throwing a load of clothes in the washer, and finally collapsing into bed.

Peppy Peggy greets her husband at the door, bathed and smelling of fresh perfume. Dinner is ready and includes a hot loaf of his favorite bread with a jar of last summer's homemade strawberry preserves. After dinner she spends quality time with him and the children, having completed her "home work" earlier in the day.

Which do you think a husband prefers to see upon arriving home in the evening? Which woman has the best chance of cheerfully serving the Lord? Which woman has the best opportunity to balance the family budget? Which woman likely will have the calm and gentle spirit? And under which circumstances will the children have the best prospects of being brought up "in the discipline and instruction of the Lord?" (See Ephesians 6:4 RSV.)

8: Avoiding the Newlywed Squeeze

Would you like some fatherly advice from an experienced bill collector? Would you like some positive, practical tips you can take to ensure that your marriage will not suffer from financial problems? Set a goal *now* to be *financially free*.

One of the primary problems of married couples is their *failure to identify goals*. A couple without financial goals will drift very quickly into debt, buying things they want with money they don't have.

Fit To Be Tied, or Just Knotted

The average young couple I counsel have been married two or three years. Both have jobs, regular earnings, no financial goals, no budget, big debts, and plenty of arguments about money.

Not a single couple has ever told me, "Well, we did it. By our deliberate overspending, we've reached our three-year goal of owing $10,000. Our frequent arguments over money and the financial pressures we feel are just what we planned. The thrill we feel as we look forward to paying off these debts is the highlight of our marriage."

That's not what they say. They do ask, "How did it happen? Why didn't somebody tell us about debt?"

Do you know what a $10,000 debt means? Not just that they owe the credit card companies a total of $10,000. But that their monthly interest due totals $150.

Did you see that clearly? One-hundred-and-fifty-dollars a month due in interest! And the monthly payment to pay off the

$10,000 debt in four years at an 18-percent interest rate will total
$293.75. Think of it: for the next four years, 48 months, a regular
payment on their debt every month of $293.75. A total of $14,100.

When I tell the couple what it will take to pay off these debts, they
are stunned. "How will we do it? We haven't been able to make it
without making all these debt payments. How will we do it *with*
them?"

"Painfully," is my answer.

It's much better to find out that you can't afford debt payments
now, rather than after you're committed to 48 months of them.

What does it mean to be financially free? I once asked that
question of Jim Underwood, president of the National Institute of
Christian Financial Planning. His answer was that being financially
free means living without *any* of these symptoms of personal
financial problems:

- You are preoccupied with thoughts about money, at the
  expense of thoughts about God.
- You don't give what you feel God wants you to give.
- You are not at peace to live on what God has provided.
- You argue within your family about money matters.
- You can't or don't pay credit cards in full each month.
- You need or have considered a consolidation loan.
- You receive notices of past-due accounts.
- You charge items because you can't pay cash.
- You use spending as emotional therapy.
- You spend impulsively.
- You invade savings to meet current expenses.
- Your net worth does not increase annually.
- You "just can't save."
- You are underinsured.
- You wish you had a plan for spending and saving, and you're
  frustrated because you don't.

If you want to avoid any and all of these 15 symptoms, you'll set
your goal to be financially free. But it will take two *basic* decisions.
By facing these two decisions now, you are virtually assured of
getting a super-fast start on your goal of being financially free.

No debt. Decide at the outset that you will not spend what you do not have. "No money, no spendee."

Trust God instead of trusting a loan. Turn to God instead of to credit cards. You'll find God more economical and much more merciful.

Marjean and I made this decision when we were first married. We have never borrowed any money for anything other than the two houses we've bought.

Do you think we have ever for one minute regretted that decision? We have not. And we've never been sorry that we'vc had no debt payments to include in our annual budget.

Marjean's 2¢: Young Couples CAN Live Within Their Means

When our oldest daughter Jenny and her husband Greg were married, they lived in a basement apartment furnished with an old couch the school provided, a borrowed bed, a bean-bag chair, a small table and two chairs. When they finished school and found jobs, their incomes were small. So they didn't have much when they moved out of the school housing into another basement apartment. It was amazing for us to sec how frugally they lived and saved their money. We were excited when their better jobs earned them enough money to move into a real upstairs apartment.

In the house George and I built in 1957, wc didn't have enough furniture for both the family room and living room, so we left the living room bare: no furniture and no carpet, drapes, or light fixtures.

Much later, the friend who sold us our air conditioner (which we waited to put in the house 'til the next summer, when we had the cash) remarked, "Well, one thing about you two: You have lived what you've talked. I remember over 20 years ago, when I came out to your house to figure your air conditioner needs, and you didn't have a stick of furniture in your living room. George said he'd rather be cool than have furniture."

People watch our lives. Do we measure up? Do our lives help or hinder our testimony?

Keep Records

Talk over and decide now how you plan to spend your income. Set up a written budget. (Details are presented in later chapters.)

Decide from this day forward that you will include in your monthly spending plan each of these goals: 1) giving, 2) saving, 3) spending.

GIVING. You and I, who are God's people, are to be funnels of God's flow of resources. The Bible says, "Give, and it will be given to you..." (Luke 6:38 RSV). When the spout is blocked at the bottom because of our stinginess, God can put nothing else in at the top.

Young couples often feel they just don't have enough to give now. With their incomes low and their desires for furniture and stuff to fill the place where they live, there's just no money to give to the Lord. Such an analysis will prove there's not enough to give and buy all those other things.

Giving to the Lord is not so much a matter of money as it is trusting God. When we give to the Lord first, we are really telling Him we have the faith that He will replace it with more than enough to meet our needs. As our needs are met, we'll continue to be His channel for giving resources to others.

Are you trustworthy with what God has given you? Do you acknowledge that everything you have has come because God has made it possible?

A first-off-the-top-of-your-income tithe is the best way I know to prove to yourself and to demonstrate to God that you trust Him. One of my friends says God is the only business manager in the world who can make 90 percent go farther than 100 percent.

Start your marriage as tithers. Know the joy and blessing of giving to others as you start your life learning to give to each other in marriage.

The outflow of money from your new marriage will add to your relationship a certain rare quality that will be meaningful to you and attractive to others.

SAVING. The excuses for not saving are the same as the

reasons for not giving. With income low and desires high, right now is not the time to save.

Where giving is an act of faith, saving must be a habit of pay days. Paying yourself second (tithe is first) will ensure that you regularly add to a small savings that will grow continually. Such savings will be your "never-to-spend" money. This money will be working for you each day of your life. If your never-to-spend savings were to total just $25 every month for 40 years, and if that savings earned five percent per year, you'd have $38,411 in 40 years. At that time you could leave it in at five-percent interest and withdraw $160 a month, without touching the $38,411. Or you could withdraw $406 a month for 10 years before your funds were exhausted.

I've never seen a couple who ever regretted their decision to save money regularly. But I've seen hundreds of folks who wished they had started the savings habit before it was too late.

You also will need some savings to spend. Careful planning will have you save regularly, in advance, for purchases in the future. Such items as cars, furniture, major appliances, and college educations are items for which you can save.

Saving for major purchases rather than financing them immediately can save you large amounts of money. However, most people do not save for purchases such as a new car. They tell me they just can't save for a car. So they justify financing the purchase of a car.

That's not right thinking. One of my definitions for debt is: "savings in reverse, plus interest."

Can you imagine how much money Marjean and I have saved over the years by saving in advance for every purchase? Our savings came from several resources:

- Interest earned while we saved to buy the item.
- Interest not paid because of debt.
- Bargains we took advantage of because we had the cash.
- The natural restraint we exercised in most purchases, because we didn't plan to spend more money for the item than we had saved for it.

Decide now to *save* for everything you ever buy. You'll save in more ways than one. You'll save arguments, frustration, stresses and strains, as well as interest.

SPENDING. A careful budget will be a boon to your spending. Just having a plan and then keeping records will bring huge rewards to you financially.

Here are some practical money-saving tips to help you during those first years of marriage.

Limit your eating out. Don't let anybody tell you it's cheaper than eating at home.

Restaurant industry figures show that food costs account for only 30 percent of total expenses. In your own apartment, you don't pay extra for the rent, advertising, insurance, taxes, clean-up, security, and labor that restaurants incur. You don't buy menus or extra dishes and glasses, or pay the cook and meal server. Those items—and many more—are included in the price of every meal you eat out.

Limit your TV watching. Dr. Ed Wheat, Christian physician and author, developed a reputation as one of the country's leading authorities on physical intimacy in marriage. In his premarital counseling, his two pieces of advice for the first year of marriage were formulated to enhance the couple's sexual relationship:

1) "Don't borrow money for any reason."
2) "Don't own a television set."

You should discuss these decisions together and see how you think they could affect your relationship with each other.

Learn to create together. When you have a need, such as table and chairs, be creative in locating other people's junk. (They sell their junk cheap.) Their junk can become your treasure.

Visualize what some repairs can mean to that old wood table. Picture how beautiful the top will be when you've filled in those holes and sanded the table down to its natural beauty. And think how pleased you'll be with this table when it's been stained or painted to blend in with your own home.

Marjean and I are still eating and serving meals to friends on a table we bought for $30 years ago. I'm still amazed that the antiquing job she did with less than $15 worth of supplies turned that junk table into an item of furniture that looks so nice in our home.

Limit your driving. How many people do you know who have a mileage budget for their cars?

Driving costs money. The more miles you drive, the more money you spend. The more you drive, the sooner you will need new tires and car repairs.

Find ways to cut your driving! Combine trips for shopping, visits, and entertainment. Enjoy days at home, when you never get in your car. Learn to use public transportation. Learn to walk and ride bikes.

✗ We have a shopping mall that is exactly a 20-minute walk from our home. We enjoy walking there together to buy things we need. Seldom do we buy more than we need; carrying it home on the 20-minute walk could be a real burden.

Keep a predetermined amount of money with you. The total amount of money we had with us for the first 40 years of marriage was never more than $40. Our billfolds each were planned to be stocked with two $20 bills.

Whatever I spent of that $40 had to be replaced from our petty cash envelopes at home. Knowing how much I originally had with me helped me determine what I'd bought with the amount that was spent but not recorded.

Include a small allowance for yourselves. A monthly amount of $10 to $40 should be yours to spend for whatever you want. I've used mine for haircuts, golf games, football tickets, a super sundae, magazines, and hundreds of other items. Marjean is delighted with these expenditures, because she knows they are part of the budget and I'm not overspending our money when I blow my allowance.

Don't own a pet. Please don't report me to the Society for the Prevention of Cruelty to Animals. The fact that our little dachshund lived to be 17 partially resulted, I'm certain, from the daily walks she and I took during the last three years of her life.

Pets are expensive. Cat and dog food isn't cheap. When animals get hurt, most people take them to the vet. They weren't meant to exist in carpeted and draped homes, and they often cause considerable damage to home furnishings. Animal care when you travel is expensive.

One of our friends dog-sits every day for her daughter and son-in-law's dog while they work. She refers to the little dog as "Granddog."

The night our daughter Amy and her fiancé shared their wedding desires with Marjean and me, we had a real laugh. After we had expressed our agreement with their hopes, Amy said, "Hey, Mom and Dad, we have a wedding present for you: Chaussee! Mike doesn't like cats." We'd been keeping Amy's kitty at home during her four years of college. Now, Chaussee looks like a permanent fixture.

I also enjoy a beautiful keeshond named Elka. Every evening Elka comes to our back door, and I let her in. We talk and bark, romp, and have a great time. Then I give her one dog biscuit, and she leaves. When Marjean and I go on walks, Elka joins us. We all have a ball.

Elka belongs to our next-door neighbor. I let him buy the food, pay the vet bills and be awakened around 5 a.m. every day to let Elka out. What a neat way to enjoy a dog.

Pray together about financial decisions. When counseling a couple in money trouble, I frequently ask if they're praying together. Not just about money, but about everything.

Very few couples know the blessing that comes with prayer in marriage. But the Bible is full of promises about the special power that comes from the Lord when two pray together. Jesus Himself gave us one of those promises: "Again I say to you, if two of you agree on earth about anything they ask, it will be done for them by my Father in heaven. For where two or three are gathered in my name, there am I in the midst of them" (Matthew 18:19, 20 RSV).

What more welcome place to have that special presence of God than in your young marriage relationship? As Marjean and I have prayed together, the Lord has blessed our praying, our relationship and our home in a very special way. Our prayer would be for your marriage to start financially free and to be fruitful in God's sight.

9: Budgeting Helps Unsqueeze Us

Roger and Debbie had $20 in the bank, no savings, and last month's house payment three weeks past due. Even with both of them working, their next two paychecks would not stretch far enough to pay two house payments, overdue utility bills, food to eat, and gas for the car.

They panicked, and Debbie called me for an appointment.

Their financial summary may shock you, but it was no surprise to me. I've counseled dozens of young couples who are both working and who have messes like this.

Everyone who comes to me for financial counseling must fill out a financial summary before I begin helping them. Roger and Debbie's is shown on the next page.

With 32 months of marriage behind them, two good jobs, a $60,000 house in their name, and driving only one small, not-so-new car between them, you'd think they would be in excellent financial shape.

Not so! Otherwise, they wouldn't be in my office seeking help.

A Panicky Present

I started with the usual question: "What is your problem?"

Roger answered, "I think we have too much debt, but I don't think we have more than anybody else."

"What have you done about your problem?" I asked.

"Well, we've prayed about it and talked a lot about it."

81

Financial Summary

Date _____

A. What We Own (Assets):
   1. Money in the bank $ 20
   2. Cash value of life insurance
      (call agent on each policy)   _____
   3. Savings (savings & loan,
      credit union, etc.)   _____
   4. Stocks & bonds
      (present market value)   _____
   5. Real estate
      a. Home (price home would
         readily sell for on today's market)   60,000
      b. Other real estate   _____
   6. Other investments   _____
   7. Personal possessions (for each
      room you have that is nicely
      furnished, multiply by $1,000)   4,000
   8. Automobiles (call dealer, ask for
      average retail price of your car/cars)   5,000
   9. Other property (boats, trailers,
      cabins, etc.)   _____
   10. Special property (cameras, guns,
       hobbies, motorcycles, silver,
       camping equipment, electronics)   _____
   11. Interest in retirement or pension plan   _____

What We Own Totals
   (1–4) Cash & other savings   20
   (5) Real estate   60,000
   (6–11) Other property   9,000
Grand Total of What We Own $69,020

	Amount Due	Monthly Payment	Estm. Annual Interest
B. What We Owe			
1. To the mortgagor of our home	$49,180	488.00	9%
2. To others	300	25.00	18%
a. Parents	1,250	71.24	12%
b. Bank	1,335	53.00	28%
c. Credit union	2,450	100.00	12%
d. Insur. companies	0	34.25	?
3. Credit cards	750	48.00	18%
4. Other businesses	60	11.00	18%
5. Other – school loan	2,700	35.00	7%
6. Medical or dental	576		
Grand Total, What We Owe	$58,601	$865.49	

A Planless Past

So I asked them the same question I've asked every couple and person who has come to me for financial counsel: "Do you have a written plan for your spending? Do you have a budget?"

And I heard the same answer I've always heard. "No." (The only deviation from that blunt answer has been the occasional couple who say, "We tried that once, but it didn't work.")

I started adding up the debt figures they had brought in on the financial summary. The total came to $9,421, not counting the $49,180 house mortgage.

Then I told them I was subtracting the $2,700 they brought to the marriage in school loans and the $1,250 her father had loaned them to help with the down payment on their house. The new total of $5,471 in debt was the amount by which they had overspent their income during their 32 months of marriage.

They could hardly believe they'd overspent by $171 a month. It didn't help much when I told them, "A panicky present is the result of a planless past. Your planless past has caught up with you. Without records and with credit cards, it has been very easy for you to plunge into the debt trap. But it won't be as easy to escape."

Roger and Debbie had done what came naturally. Roger was right: They probably weren't any more in debt than most couples their age who didn't determine, at marriage, to keep out of debt and to keep records.

A little boy was asked in Sunday school if he knew the definition of a *budget*. He said, "Yeah, I know what that is: It's a family argument."

Marjean and I have found just the opposite. With a plan for our spending that includes room for car and household repairs, that counts on taxes and insurance, and that allows for some vacation time together as a family, we haven't faced the panicky present.

Oftentimes an unexpected financial problem leads us to the budget book to look at the facts together. We find what we can do without, what we can say *no* to in order to say *yes* to the present emergency. It is a matter of prayer and of choice between alternatives.

With no spending plan, the choices are not clear. In the maze of confusion, most couples argue about what to do, and then just charge the problem. The increased payments and interest lead to more financial pressures and more frequent arguments.

Budgeting — What Is It?

Budgeting is planned spending. Doesn't that sound easy?

And budgeting *is* easy when you understand its purpose, follow a workable system and use it to maximize the family income. A family who know where their money is going usually can make it go farther.

Most of the money you earn in your life, you will spend. You will spend your funds for things you want. Unfortunately, your yearnings will exceed your earnings.

If you follow your wants in your buying, the result will be chaos. If you design your spending, then your dollars can take care of you. With a system, you probably will be more satisfied, have more of what you really want, and have fewer financial problems. Without a strategy, money matters probably will cause tension and crisis in your family.

A careful airplane pilot checks the supply of gas before every trip. The journey is plotted with care, to make certain there will be gas enough to reach the destination. The pilot usually makes certain enough gas is held in reserve to allow a diversion to another airport in case of bad weather at the planned destination. Federal Aviation Agency regulations require such planning on all instrument flights. Good sense requires such foresight on every flight.

You, as a spender, also will reach more financial destinations through careful, disciplined, and planned spending — budgeting.

When each of our two daughters started kindergarten, she began her first budget. The mechanical system consisted of three small boxes of the same size, stapled together. Each box was labeled by category and marked by amount: SAVE, SPEND, and CHURCH.

Every week I parceled out the allowance: three nickels. One went into each box. The budget was evident, the plan simple. Visual control was established. Even a 6-year-old began to understand her planned spending.

The three-box method was adequate through high school. The amounts changed as the girls grew and as inflation roared, but the boxes continued in use as a control system. Intriguingly, the girls were seldom out of money. When they were, they knew it. No money in the box meant no money to spend!

Here's a real lesson for those who continually plunge into debt by spending more than they have. A budget is the best way I know to avoid the pitfall of too much month left over at the end of your money.

There is more to budgeting than simply planning your spending. Check-ups are essential to compare the money you spend with your budget. Whether you use small boxes to maintain visual control or a budget book to record spending, you need a record-keeping system. The principle of record keeping is well established in the Bible by this verse: "Any enterprise is built by wise planning, becomes strong through common sense and profits wonderfully by keeping abreast of the facts" (Proverbs 24:3, 4 TLB). Let's break that down:

ANY ENTERPRISE. That marriage is an enterprise may be a surprise. It is easy for you to add up the income from your previous years of employment. You can project your expected earnings for the years between now and retirement. Consider inflation in your figures, allowing a three- to five-percent annual inflation rate. That your earning and spending form a financial enterprise is a fact which your figures will demonstrate clearly.

WISE PLANNING. Salespeople are counseled to "plan the work and work the plan." This is good counsel for those seeking to follow God's principle of record keeping. How are your records? Where has your planning taken you?

Completion of the financial summary sheet (a blank one is found at the end of this chapter) will help you determine the present state of your financial affairs. Your net worth is calculated as the total of what you own (total assets) minus the total of what you owe (total liabilities). When you have figured your net worth, you may consider how many years have been required to accumulate your resources. You can determine how much you have added each year to your financial net worth.

COMMON SENSE. "Can two walk together, except they be agreed?" (Amos 3:3 KJV). Agreement in the spending plan for the family is essential for the husband and wife. Seldom do I see a family with financial problems where there is not real tension within the marriage.

Common sense dictates common goals, which demand common effort and produce uncommon results. God's multiplication system for working together equals abundant results: "Two can accomplish more than twice as much as one, for the results can be much better" (Ecclesiastes 4:9). "Work happily together" is the first requisite for the family spending plan. (See Romans 12:16.)

KEEPING ABREAST. A friend of mine says you keep a budget so you won't fake yourself out. How can you plug the leaks in the budget if you don't know where the leaks are? Would you be satisfied if you were in the hospital with heart trouble and no one bothered to check up on your blood pressure, pulse count, and temperature?

I have seldom seen people who were successful stewards of their money who did not keep good records. And I rarely see a couple in financial trouble who are operating on a spending plan with adequate records.

Some years ago our company contracted with a telephone company for 10 hours of long-distance time each month. For that minimum we paid a flat rate plus a charge for each additional minute of use over the 10 hours. All employees were aware of the objective of avoiding usage in excess of the 10 hours. I started them all out with this admonition: "Do the best you can."

Here are the results, in round figures, for the first three months: 13 hours of use for the first month, 16 hours for the second month, 19 hours for the third month. By the end of the third month we were using almost twice the time for which we'd budgeted.

My plan had failed; it was time for a better system. We then instituted individual responsibility. Each employee had an allotted number of minutes to use during the month. The employee was to keep track of his or her accumulated usage for the month. A chart was devised to show our total daily usage, with everyone advised as to where we were, compared to where we planned to be. Keeping abreast of these facts, and using discipline to stay within individual quotas, our usage dropped back to 10 hours for the fourth month and didn't exceed 12 hours monthly thereafter. Record keeping allowed us to meet our objective.

As a teen-ager, my daughter Jenny once asked me, "Dad, why are we so poor? It seems I can never buy the clothes I want, and neither can Mom." My response was a lengthy lecture on how we chose to spend our income. Finally, I explained that our family operated on a clothing budget and that there simply was not enough money budgeted to buy at *all* times *all* the clothes *all* of us wanted.

Jenny pressed further. "How come I can't have my own budget?" Marjean and I discussed this idea privately and decided to open checking accounts for each of the teen-age girls. Monthly we would deposit the budgeted amount into their accounts. They were to pay for all their own clothes as they bought them. Checks were not to be written on these accounts, except for their clothes.

Prior to the personal budgeting, we'd had horrendous arguments whenever we'd said no to clothing purchases. With the responsibility shifted to each daughter and with a predetermined plan, arguments stopped.

After a few tough lessons learned from purchasing items that were too expensive and running out of money for real needs, both girls became excellent shoppers. What better way to "train up a child in the way he should go" financially than to provide an opportunity for individual responsibility in decisions on teen-age clothes?

The goal of such training for children is to steadily increase the financial responsibility they have. By learning individual responsibility for money, the young person is being well prepared to leave the nest.

Before you as parents can teach God's principles for money to your children, you must have attended classes yourselves. Whether you are struggling with debt or have some financial success, *you can profit* and God can reap from your keeping a budget.

Financial Summary

Date _____

A. **What We Own (Assets):**
1. Money in the bank _____
2. Cash value of life insurance
    (call agent on each policy) _____
3. Savings (savings & loan,
    credit union, etc.) _____
4. Stocks & bonds
    (present market value) _____
5. Real estate
    a. Home (price home would
    readily sell for on today's market) _____
    b. Other real estate _____
6. Other investments _____
7. Personal possessions (for each
    room you have that is nicely
    furnished, multiply by $1,000) _____
8. Automobiles (call dealer, ask for
    average retail price of your car/cars) _____
9. Other property (boats, trailers,
    cabins, etc.) _____
10. Special property (cameras, guns,
    hobbies, motorcycles, silver,
    camping equipment, electronics) _____
11. Interest in retirement or pension plan _____

What We Own Totals
    (1–4) Cash & other savings
    (5) Real estate _____
    (6–11) Other property _____
Grand Total of What We Own _____

	Amount Due	Monthly Payment	Estm. Annual Interest
B. What We Owe			
1. To the mortgagor of our home	___	___	___
2. To others			
a. Bank	___	___	___
b. Credit union	___	___	___
c. Insur. companies	___	___	___
3. Credit cards	___	___	___
4. Other businesses	___	___	___
5. Other (family loans, etc.)	___	___	___
6. Medical or dental	___	___	___
Grand Total, What We Owe			___

10: Budget Details — A Priceless Prescription For Preservation

You need to take three steps to establish and maintain your budget:

1. *Plan your spending.*
2. *Balance your budget.*
3. *Start keeping records.*

PLAN YOUR SPENDING. Fill out the financial goals sheet (next page). Make estimates of what you need and want to spend in each category. If the spending is monthly, multiply by 12 to get the annual figure; if the spending is yearly, divide by 12 to get the monthly amount.

Use the following "Notes For Our Financial Goals" to stimulate your thinking in each area. Review the last 12 months' check stubs to get the amounts you spent for the items listed. Enter a monthly amount for any additional category you have (items 19–21). Whatever extras you cannot afford, such as a vacation, leave out.

List all debt payments, excluding the car payment and house mortgage payment, under debt reduction. Include the house payment under "shelter" and the car payment under "transportation."

NOTES FOR OUR FINANCIAL GOALS

These explanations for each category will guide you in arriving at amounts for each spending category. Start with Number 1 and work through them in order. Remember that a journey of 1,000 miles begins with the first step.

Our Financial Goals

		Monthly	Annually
1.	Tithes and offerings		
2.	Federal income tax		
3.	State income tax		
4.	Social Security tax		
5.	Other taxes (such as city)		
6.	Shelter		
7.	Food		
8.	Clothing		
9.	Health		
10.	Education		
11.	Life insurance		
12.	Gifts		
13.	Transportation		
14.	Personal allowances		
15.	Vacations		
16.	Savings		
17.	Household purchases		
18.	Debt reduction		
19.			
20.			
21.			
Totals			

1. *Tithes and offerings*: all charitable giving—church, United Way, etc.
2. *Federal income tax*: all amounts withheld, estimates paid, and any amounts due with tax returns.
3. *State income tax*: all amounts withheld, estimates paid, and any amounts due with tax returns.
4. *Social Security tax*: all amounts withheld.
5. *Other taxes*: taxes on your wages, such as city income tax.

6. *Shelter*: if renting, includes rent, heat, lights, telephone, household supplies, appliance repairs, magazine and newspaper subscriptions, and other home-related expenses; if buying, includes house payments, interest, insurance, real estate taxes, repairs and maintenance, and other items listed under renting.

7. *Food*: grocery store items, paper goods, cleaning supplies, pet foods; includes all eating out, carry-out items, and school lunches; also may include entertainment.

8. *Clothing*: purchases, cleaning, repairs; may be divided with a separate budget for each family member.

9. *Health*: health insurance premiums, medical, dental, hospital expenses, drug items, medicines, and cosmetics.

10. *Education*: school supplies, books, lessons, college expenses, uniforms, and equipment.

11. *Life insurance*: all premiums, whether paid monthly, quarterly, or annually.

12. *Gifts*: birthdays, anniversaries, special occasions, Christmas, weddings, funerals, office collections, and dues for organizations.

13. *Transportation*: gas, oil, repairs, licenses, personal property tax, and insurance; includes car payments or an amount set aside to purchase your next car.

14. *Personal allowances*: for each family member to spend personally — hair care, recreation, baby-sitting, hobbies, and children's allowances.

15. *Vacations*: trips, camps, and weekend outings; trips for weddings, funerals, and family visits.

16. *Savings*: amounts set aside now for future needs.

17. *Household purchases*: major appliances, furniture, carpeting and major home maintenance such as roofing and painting.

18. *Short-term debt reduction*: all payments on debt not included in other categories, such as school loans and amounts due to relatives, banks, or others.

19–21. *Special categories*: anything tailored to your own needs or desires; may include a boat, cabin, airplane, or hobby items.

BALANCE YOUR BUDGET. When you add up your spending plan, you'll be most unusual if the total amount you plan to spend does not exceed your income. The spending often comes to several hundred dollars each month above the net income.

You've probably just discovered what most people don't learn until it is too late. You've seen in black and white that if you spend the minimum you think it will take to live, you'll be going into debt every month. That's the easy way it happens to most folks.

One of my friends used to think a budget was a way of showing him he couldn't live on what he made. Now he realizes a budget is to help him be able to live on what he makes.

Do you know any way you can be more personally involved in your own life than to try to balance a budget that is out of whack by, say, $200 a month? Communication between husband and wife must be practically forced; choices must be dealt with; involvement in your lives is assured, as you work out the realities of your spending plan. You'll have to cut, trim, shrink, slice, shave, reduce, curtail, and carve dollars everywhere to reduce that spending.

But as a Christian, you have hope. So pray now. Ask the Lord to open your eyes and heart to His leading.

He wants to meet your *needs.* Jesus gave you a tremendous promise: "What is impossible with men is possible with God" (Luke 18:27 RSV).

Now open your eyes and look at your financial goals again. Start asking questions such as these:

• *Shelter*: Can we afford this place? Shelter should not require more than 30 percent of your gross income. If your gross income is $3,000 monthly, all expenses for shelter should not exceed $900. If you are over in this area, you may need to secure a cheaper living situation in order to balance your budget.

• *Food*: Is eating out eating up our food budget? How much money a month could we save with weekly menu planning? Food should not require more than 7 to 15 percent of your monthly income (the greater the income, the less the percentage for food).

• *Clothing*: Have we prayed specifically for all needs to be met with bargains? Have we explored the good used clothing stores and tried the garage sales in expensive neighborhoods? Clothing should take no more than 3 to 4 percent of your income.

• *Health*: Would regular exercise cut our doctor bills? How much could be saved in unnecessary dental bills if junk foods were eliminated?

• *Education*: Are those lessons really necessary?

• *Life insurance*: Can whole life be switched to term insurance?

• *Gifts*: What creative family projects can be started to give meaningful one-of-a-kind gifts?

• *Transportation*: How much debt and monthly expense could be saved through the sale of our best car? By reducing driving by 20 percent?

• *Personal allowance*: How much would we save if each of us had a firm limit on cash spent each week for candy, pop, coffee, magazines, and "stuff?"

• *Vacations*: Should our family vacation this year be a time of earning, instead of giving in to our yearnings?

• *Household purchases*: Have we tried the garage sales for our absolute needs? (After praying, of course!)

• *Debt reduction*: Just picture no more payments! *Ever*! Now SQUEEZE all you can for those debt payments. How much could you add to your debt payments if you worked in your neighborhood, for church members, on Saturdays?

Your short-term debt should not exceed 10 percent of your monthly take-home pay times 18. With a monthly net income of $2,500, the debt limit would be $250 times 18 equals $4,500. This figure would not include a mortgage on your home. The experts say you are headed for trouble if your short-term monthly debt payments exceed 20 percent of your take-home pay. Thus, with a take-home pay of $2,500, you are in real financial trouble if your monthly payments for debt exceed $500, excluding a home mortgage.

Put the pencil to the answers to those questions and the eraser to your first figures. Keep figuring and erasing until the budget balances (income equals expenses) and you have the peace of God in your heart about your spending plan.

To stimulate your own thinking, I've included a sample budget (next page) for a family of four trying to balance a debt-free budget on a $45,000 annual gross income. Use it as a starting point for working out your own spending plan.

Sample Budget
(Husband, Age 34; Wife, Age 34; Children, 10 & 8)

Our Financial Goals

		Monthly	Annually	Percent Of Income
1.	Tithes and offerings	$ 375	$ 4,500	10%
2.	Federal income tax	375	4,500	10%
3.	State income tax	113	1,350	3%
4.	Social Security tax	300	3,600	8%
5.	Other taxes (*i.e.*, city)			
6.	Shelter *	938	11,250	25%
7.	Food	563	6,750	15%
8.	Clothing	150	1,800	4%
9.	Health	150	1,800	4%
10.	Education	38	450	1%
11.	Life insurance	38	450	1%
12.	Gifts	75	900	2%
13.	Transportation **	413	4,950	11%
14.	Personal allowances	75	900	2%
15.	Vacations			
16.	Savings	150	1,800	4%
17.	Household purchases			
18.	Debt reduction			
19.				
20.				
21.				
Totals		$3,753	$45,000	100%

* Shelter includes the mortgage payment on the house, real estate tax, personal property taxes, and related taxes.

** Transportation costs for two cars include gas, repairs, insurance, taxes, and car replacement; the assumption is that they are driven a total of 20,000 miles annually at a fraction under 25 cents per mile.

START KEEPING RECORDS. The purpose of keeping records is to see how you're doing compared to your plan.

One way to maintain a good family budget would be to open 13 different checking accounts at the bank. Each account would represent a different spending category. Out of each pay check you would deposit up to your spending plan in each account.

For example, if you planned to spend $800 a month in shelter, you'd deposit $800 during the month in your shelter checking account. As you wrote checks for your rent or house payment, utilities, repairs and household supplies, you'd list the checks on your check register and subtract the amounts from your balance in the bank. Shelter purchases might include paint, weed killer, light bulbs, flashlight batteries, floor wax, a broom, etc.

At the end of the month you'd know these two things: how much you spent for shelter according to your plan, and where you spent the money.

Don't panic! I'm not really telling you to open 13 checking accounts. I'm illustrating what you are doing when you keep a budget. Instead of 13 checking accounts, you can keep one checking account. Your budget book will have 13 spending accounts in which you show deposits for the amounts you intend to spend in each area. (You list the checks that are to be charged to each spending account.) By subtracting each check listed from the amount you planned to spend, you can see at all times how you are doing, compared to your plan.

That's what budgeting is all about. That's planned spending. That's telling your money where you want it to go, instead of wondering where it went.

Most office supply stores carry financial record books with lined columns. Your local Christian bookstore may have more elaborate planning guides that include biblical encouragements and specific instructions. Several simple, excellent personal financial programs are available for the computer.

If you have been motivated to start a budget, don't put it off. Let me encourage you with a fun portion of Scripture: "Then the Lord said to Moses, 'Quit praying and get the people moving! Forward, march!' " (Exodus 14:15 TLB).

Get started now! The debts you pay will be your own. The tithe you give will be a blessing. The budget you balance will bring peace to your heart and joy to your life.

"The desire accomplished is sweet to the soul. . . ." (Proverbs 13:19 KJV).

Marjean's 2¢: Husbands, Wives, & Budgets

I remember feeling very "put upon" when George asked me to post to the budget book. Complaining thoughts raced through my mind. "What do I know about *his* budget?" "I'll make mistakes." "I don't have time to do that." "That's *his* thing!"

Unwillingly, I said I'd do it to "help him out, this time." I did make mistakes. Math and I were never on good terms. I really had a hang-up in that area. I felt guilty when he patiently taught me how to do it and never jumped me when he found mistakes, as I thought he would do. With his tender but firm encouragement, I gained more confidence. A friend of mine calls that being "tough yet tender" — tough enough to stick to his guns, but tender in his teaching.

Before I knew it, I was given more responsibility in keeping our finances in order. Each of our jobs is equally important. We simply assume different roles.

Some of you wives may realize you have had more training in this area, so you can handle it more easily than your husbands. Remember, it took you a long time to learn finances, so your husband needs time and understanding from you. It is God's plan for the man to be the head of the home, and finance is one important area for him to carry out God's plan (see 1 Corinthians 11:3). As his helpmeet, you can help him assume his God-given role. Remember that he will become stronger as you lean on him.

I constantly hear women say their husbands never pay any attention to the finances, but leave it all to them. On questioning each woman closely, I discover that early in their marriage, she made her husband feel he was incompetent, or she refused to pay attention to his attempt at regulating their spending, so he gave up. In most families, each partner goes his or her own way, and the couple usually follow the way of debt, arguing, and misery.

We've had struggles in our marriage. I remember a New Year's Eve when George chose to look over our budget. The evening was ruined as I dissolved in tears when we discovered *I* had gone over in the food category. I hadn't kept close watch on the budget book to let it help me stay within our plan.

Furthermore, I was defensive and felt George was criticizing me. All the budget book was, in the beginning, was a record of what we spent rather than an indicator of how we were doing on our spending plan. Now, I realize George and I need to use the budget book to guide us.

As we have learned to communicate better in this area, each of our responsibilities has been determined. My responsibilities have developed into:

• paying the bills on time (I have a special box where the bills are placed when they arrive, until bill-paying time).

• keeping an accurate check stub and a running balance in the checkbook. (I am careful to write the exact amount of the check on the stub, rather than rounding up or down. Don't laugh — some do!)

• filing the receipts in an organized way. An expanding alphabetized file box is very handy.

• reconciling the bank statement soon after it arrives, to make sure the checkbook and bank agree.

• posting the checks to the categories in the budget book.

• being willing to ask George for help in checking the

budget book regularly, so he can keep abreast of the condition of each category. We are in this together, so we need to work together.

• being committed to the plan. This last responsibility is extremely important, for I believe it is workable and helpful. If I am faithful in carrying it out, it will work. In our case, our responsibilities are divided, in that I keep track of the outgo and George keeps track of the income and of me. And we've done this by mutual agreement.

In keeping this kind of budget for our spending over the years, I have reaped great benefits. Record keeping has restrained spending. For example, I resisted that beautiful leather purse, because it was not in the budget. By cleaning and polishing the old one, I found it would do just as well.

The budget has helped me become my husband's helpmeet in an important area. As most couples will admit, to be able to talk openly in the area of family finances is helpful in building a good foundation for communication.

Our children not only witnessed God's principles and the technique in action, but they also saw Mom and Dad work together in the vital area of marriage.

I also recognize that this careful training has helped prepare me for widowhood. I must face the fact that statistics show the average wife lives longer than her husband. I'm thankful I won't face those years afraid I don't know how to handle money.

By being good stewards of what God has entrusted to us, we have been able to give more to our Lord and to His work. I've had to learn to be a "cheerful giver." It has taken time for me to understand that the following verse does work practically: "And God is able to provide you with every blessing in abundance, so that you may always have enough of everything and may provide in abundance for every good work" (2 Corinthians 9:8 RSV). There's no question our budget has been one of God's great blessings. He has given me the power to be obedient to His will.

> You, too, can experience God's blessings in this area. Are
> you willing to be obedient to Him? Are you like the wise woman
> of Proverbs 14:1 (TLB) who " . . . builds her house . . . " (by
> keeping a budget) or like the foolish woman who " . . . tears hers
> down by her own efforts?"

A Surgical Process

During the energy crisis of the mid-1970s, we learned that we could
reduce heat, light, driving and recreation without serious effects on
the quality of our living. Since most of us eat too much for our own
good, a reduction in food consumption actually can lead to improved
health. Steak or hamburgers cooked by the husband on the grill at
home occasionally, served by candlelight, can be even more enjoyable
than a meal out — and far more economical.

Family togetherness can be enhanced by spending an evening
making gifts in assembly line fashion for Christmas and other
occasions. Just before Christmas a college student from our church
told me she had made her own presents. She said on a college
student's budget she couldn't afford to buy them. Her estimate was
that 10 gifts could be made for the money it took to buy one.

Spending for Christmas and special occasions very often blows
the family budget. In a family of four, one gift for each occasion —
Christmas, birthdays, anniversaries, Valentine's Day, and Easter —
easily can add up to 18 to 24 gifts. When you add the relatives and
friends, you can be involved in purchasing up to 50 presents a year.
Using family talents in creative projects can result in substantial
financial savings while you are giving to others a one-of-a-kind
expression of your love.

Major changes may be necessary in your family patterns. One
friend had accumulated four weeks of vacation each year. He also
had accumulated substantial debt. Part of the overspending was
caused by his family's concept that a vacation meant trips out of town
— with the resultant costs of driving, eating out, motels, recreation,
and purchases of curios. That family needed to plan creative
vacations where additional family income could be earned, home

maintenance could be accomplished, and creative money-saving projects could be completed. Visualize the difference in long-term family welfare between those two contrasting types of vacations.

Yes, the surgical process of trimming the family budget is painful. So is the Christian walk! Jesus instructed us clearly about the way we choose in every area of our lives: "Enter by the narrow gate; for the gate is wide and the way is easy, that leads to destruction, and those who enter by it are many. For the gate is narrow and the way is hard, that leads to life, and those who find it are few" (Matthew 7:13, 14 RSV).

The wide financial path is easy: no money down and an easy payment plan. Buy what you want when you want it. CHARGE IT! Don't bother with budgets and record keeping. Such thinking maps out the road to destruction.

God's financial way is hard. Self-denial, discipline, and sacrifice are the marks of a Christian managing money. God's stewardship calls for wise and knowledgeable use of our money. This means a plan and records to help you stay within the plan. God's abundance is not found in overspending what He provides for us, but in His blessing us as we are faithful with what He gives us.

Keep praying and cutting until your expenses are within your income. Remember: If your spending plan won't work on paper, it won't work — period.

11: S'more Unsqueezables

Do you remember those campfires where you ate s'mores? That combination of graham crackers, chocolate bars and melted marshmallows was so tasty that you always wanted some more. Thus the name: s'mores.

Christian, what percentage of your income are you giving to the Lord now: 1, 5, 10, 20, 50 percent? Whatever you're giving now, you probably would like to give s'more. More giving results in more blessings.

These blessings include:

* *Gifts*: "Give, and it will be given to you . . ." (Luke 6:38 RSV).
* *Love*: ". . . God loveth a cheerful giver" (2 Corinthians 9:7 KJV).
* *Riches*: " . . . You will always be rich enough to be generous (2 Corinthians 9:11 NEB).
* *Joy*: "They begged us to take the money so they could share in the joy of helping the Christians in Jerusalem" (2 Corinthians 8:4 TLB).

With the cost of almost everything increasing steadily, most of us are struggling to keep our spending in line with our incomes.

And into my collection agency office march dozens of Christians who have lost the spending battle and are mired deep in the debt trap. What amount do you need each month to pay your way out of the debt trap: $50, $100, $150, $200, $300?

S'more Ways Out

With debts and inflation plaguing us, what practical, biblical steps are available to help us reduce our spending so we can dramatically increase our giving and/or our debt payments?

Did you know the Bible has principles to guide us in our spending? And each principle is a two-fold benefit: You have money saved, and you are God-blessed.

The Bible teaches, "But he who looks into the perfect law, the law of liberty, and perseveres, being no hearer that forgets but a doer that acts, he shall be blessed in his doing" (James 1:25 RSV).

If you want God's blessing on your spending, look at the biblical principles in this chapter and implement them into your own personal finances. And for each principle you obey, you may expect to cut your spending to the glory of God.

AVOID DEBT. The most frequently violated money command in Scripture in my experience is "be content with your wages" (Luke 3:14 KJV). The sure sign of violation of this Scripture is overspending your pay.

The easiest way to allow your spending to get out of control is to succumb to the minimum payment charge account and the good-almost-anywhere credit card. The only thing easy about "easy payment" is the ease of buying to accumulate large balances on your account. Most of you, along with hundreds of people I've counseled, can testify that repaying those runaway revolving accounts is tough stuff. From my vantage point, there are no entanglements more strangling than the mounting pressure of debts.

Counselees bring me glowing reports of less spending and balanced budgets, after that great family-credit-card-destruction ceremony. That's the time when you gather, as a family, to destroy all of your credit cards by cutting them into small pieces. Then you commit yourselves to one another to buy with cash only. All testify that cash spending is a real money-saving revelation.

On an installment debt of $7,000, an interest rate of 18 percent results in a *monthly interest payment* of $105.

You can see that avoiding debt may save you approximately

$105 a month. Isn't that a tremendous profit resulting from obedience to God's Word: "Owe no man any thing" (Romans 13:8 KJV)?

PLAN YOUR SPENDING. Most people don't plan their spending. Jesus instructed us to count the cost: "For which one of you, when he wants to build a tower, does not first sit down and calculate the cost, to see if he has enough to complete it?" (Luke 14:28 NAS).

The record in my counseling is unbroken. It's my experience that if you are not operating on a budget, you are wasting between $50 and several hundred dollars a month. When you've established a plan for your spending, you'll frequently find yourself using those money-saving, almost magical five little words: *It's not in the budget*!

Nowhere is planned spending more important than in certain "budget busters." Any well-managed household can turn from success to failure on any one of these three expenditures:

- Vacations
- Christmas
- Back to school

A vacation without a budget is a family disaster. Heading cross-country with no spending plan often ends with surprise debts.

One enterprising family split its vacation funds in half. All the family knew was that they would travel as long and as far as the first half of the money lasted. With the other half, they would return home. They traveled much farther than they had expected and returned home having spent no more than they had planned.

Be certain to set aside at least six cents per mile for those car repairs and tire usage that will be part of any long automobile trip. For a thousand-mile trip, you'll need $60 or more; higher-mileage trips cost proportionately more.

Families with no plan often use back-to-school desires and Christmas gift giving as times to spend without counting the cost. The obvious answer to such sprees is to set aside some money each month in special Christmas and back-to-school funds. Then discipline yourself to spend only the amount you accumulated for that specific purpose.

Charles Spurgeon said, "To earn money is easy compared with spending it well." To the servants who were wise stewards of what God had entrusted to them, the Lord said, "Well done, good and faithful servant; thou has been faithful over a few things, I will make thee ruler over many things: enter thou into the joy of the Lord" (Matthew 25:23 KJV).

Being faithful in spending what God has entrusted to you will increase your ability to give. That's a biblical principle.

AVOID WASTE. Whether wasting money through not keeping a budget or by paying interest on accumulated debt, the result is the same: violation of another scriptural principle.

What did Jesus command after the miraculous feeding of the 5,000? "Gather up the fragments that remain, that nothing be lost" (John 6:12 KJV).

Surveys reveal that approximately 10 percent of food purchases are thrown out in the garbage. How many meals a week do you eat of well-preserved, well-planned leftovers? What some people call "planover meals" may reduce your food spending by $30 to 50 per month.

Marjean's 2¢: S'mores

"*Plan*overs! Don't you mean *left*overs? Aren't you just trying to cover up last Sunday's leftovers?"

No, I truly mean planovers. When I write out my menus for the week, I plan certain days to cook more of a food than I will use for one meal. For instance, I will stew a chicken and use part of it for chicken and noodles and the rest of it, say the breast, for either chicken sandwiches or chicken divan. I can freeze the rest of the chicken for a meal I already have planned later in the week.

By doubling the meat-and-tomato sauce I make for spaghetti tonight, I can freeze the other portion for another meal of Sloppy Joes, chili, or a beef-and-macaroni casserole.

By planning my menus for a week and writing them on a month-at-a-glance calendar, I can arrange the foods to fit our activities, plus keep them varied. On Wednesday morning, when I sit down with the newspaper grocery ads, my menu calendar, and my activity calendar, I think in terms of having a casserole, an old favorite, a new recipe, and fish, chicken, and beef dishes. Many mothers, in training their daughters to cook, will give one night's dinner to them to plan and prepare. I would especially encourage this during summer vacation.

After entering the main dish on each of the days of the week, taking into consideration my activities during the day and the preparation time required, I decide what vegetable and/or salad, bread, and dessert would accompany each entrée. My decisions also would be governed by the best buys listed in the ads and what I had on hand. Then, from my menus, I would think through the ingredients needed and prepare my grocery list.

Another time saver is to picture the layout of the store and list the items in the order I come to them. This saves much back-tracking. Resist — I repeat, *resist* — impulse purchases. You haven't planned for them, and they will raise your check-out bill. Remember, they are put in that special display to entice you.

Before you leave home, estimate what your bill will be. That way you won't be surprised, and you will be in control of your budget. Have an idea what you can spend each week, and plan accordingly. Take a small calculator with you to keep check on yourself. This also will make you aware if the checker states a total that is completely out of line. They can make mistakes.

What about coupons? Clip the coupons for the items you are purchasing to your grocery list. Compare a 30-cents-off coupon on a popular brand item to the price of the store brand. Many times the store brand will be cheaper than the amount of the popular brand, even after the coupon is deducted. I recently discovered a coupon organizer. I went through all the dozens of coupons I'd clipped, tossed the outdated ones and the ones for items I never use, and alphabetized the others. Now I have them all together, ready to take to the store.

I keep the grocery list and menu calendar clipped to the

refrigerator, so I easily can add an item when I use the last one. Then I don't forget it when I'm shopping. This menu is fun for kids to be able to see; your family will scribble strange notes on a future date: *tacos* or *dog food casserole* (George's pet name for it). It means, "Hey, I'm hungry for this." Make a note of comments by the family about foods they like or don't like.

My friend Lynn has a tradition of allowing each member of the family the privilege of selecting the menu for his or her birthday dinner. Even if it is a weird combination, the rest of the family know it soon will be their turn, and they can choose whatever they want that night and won't get ribbed about it.

EXERCISE DISCIPLINE. As Christians, we're told that "Bodily exercise is all right, but spiritual exercise is much more important" (1 Timothy 4:8 TLB). Spiritual exercise is of great importance in the spending area. Our self-control muscles need flexing several times each day.

The push-ups I need to do daily are the repetition of those four little words: *I don't need it*! My own self-control exercise program includes no desserts at noon; salad lunches twice a week; no eggs at breakfast, except once a week; and no snacks between meals or before bed. Savings results: a bunch of calories and at least a few dollars a day. Monthly savings equal $50 or more.

Using the minimum savings of interest ($105), keeping records ($50), avoiding wasted food ($30), and self-control ($50), the reduced spending already adds up to $235 per month.

Are you ready for s'mores?

BUY USED. S'more savings come from buying used instead of new. You might as well get used to the word *used*. Remember that *new* lasts only one day.

Except for a house, automobiles are the biggest expenditure most families make. Note the loss of value of a car in its first seven years. Let's assume you bought a car for $14,000.

End Of year	Percentage loss new car	Loss of value	Current value
1	30%	$4,200	$9,800
2	50%	7,000	7,000
3	65%	9,100	4,900
4	75%	10,500	3,500
5	85%	11,900	2,100
6	90%	12,600	1,400
7	93%	13,020	980

Based on these calculations, if you buy a $14,000 new car and drive it five years, your car is worth only $2,100. Your cost of the car has been $11,900, or $2,380 annually. If you buy the same car when it is three or four years old, you can buy it for approximately $7,000. Driving it five years, you find it is worth $1,050. Your cost of the car has been $5,950, or $1,190 annually. If you assume added repairs will cost you $500 more than for the newer car for each of the five years, you've still saved $690 a year by buying and driving a used car. S'more savings of $58 a month (not counting the interest most folks pay to buy a new car).

As a counselor for people in financial trouble, I can tell you that most people are driving late model cars that are a real drain on family finances. As for me and my house, we buy them used and seem to get every place we need to go. Remember, dependability of machincs is determined by proper maintenance, not by age.

So many folks fit the bumper sticker: THIS IS THE LORD'S CAR; I BOUGHT IT WITH MY TITHE.

PLAN YOUR GIFT GIVING. Gift times often lead to splurging. Someone has said we should purge the urge to splurge.

How would you like to buy all the gifts you give at half price, but have them enjoyed twice as much? My older daughter and her husband taught me how: For her sister's August birthday, they bought her a ski cap that they got in March at the end-of-the-season sales. When the present was opened in August, Amy was pleased.

More enjoyment resulted when she wore her cap for the first time in January.

Buy your gifts several months before you give them. This takes planning, but pays rich dividends. Multiplying all the special occasions, family birthdays, and gifts for friends, you easily should save $20 monthly. Adding the $235 reduced spending, the used car savings ($58), and the planned giving ($20), you have a monthly savings of $313. What would $313 monthly add to your giving to the Lord — 50 percent, 100 percent? What would $313 monthly do to your debt repayments — double them, triple them?

Christians, let's do s'more self-control, record keeping, and doing without. Then we'll be blessed with more ability to spend whatever we have to the glory of God and more money to give to the Lord's wonderful works in this world.

12: Nest Eggs

When a natural or artificial egg is left in a nest to induce a hen or other bird to lay or continue laying eggs there, it is called a *nest egg*. The implication is that this egg, by virtue of its placement, will result in further production.

Someone has said everyone should have two aims in life: to make a little money first, and to make a little money last. Money set aside to last until it is needed at a future date usually is called a *nest egg*.

That a nest egg is meant to be productive is illustrated by the parable of the talents, as told by our Lord in Matthew 25:14–30. The first two men were given the most money and used that money to double their master's investment. It is interesting to note that in their cases the investments did not double without effort on their part. In verses 16 and 17 of The Living Bible we see that: "The man who received the $5,000 began immediately to buy and sell with it and soon earned another $5,000. The man with $2,000 went right to work, too, and earned another $2,000." The third man, however, hid the money he received in a hole in the ground for safekeeping. In the story he is condemned for not investing the money so it could at least have earned some interest. His reproof is in verses 26 and 27: "But his master replied, 'Wicked man! Lazy slave! Since you knew I would demand your profit, you should at least have put my money into the bank so I could have some interest.' "

Interest is not paid on money, but on what money does. Thus we see clearly the distinction between savings and investments. Savings are funds set aside out of income; they are moneys which are not spent. If the savings are hidden under the mattress, they continue to be savings. When those savings are entrusted to others or put to work to produce a profit or income or both, then they become an *investment*.

109

I frequently am asked about investments. These questions often deal with what I think about specific investments the inquirer has, or is interested in. These investments include such things as land, bank certificates of deposit, stocks, mutual funds, foreign currencies, gold and silver, apartments, individual retirement accounts, etc.

My answer is that I don't know about specific investments. Take land, for instance. There's ghetto land, vacant lots in neighborhoods, downtown land, prime shopping center land, suburban land, small town land, industrial land, irrigated farm land, nonirrigated farm land, resort land, forest land, desert land, mountain land, lake land, waterfront land, swamp land, unproductive land, and all other kinds of land. Whether it will be a good investment depends on how much a future buyer will want to pay for the land when the investor wants to sell. The buyers (if any are available) will depend on the potential use of the land, whether they think they can sell it for more later, and myriad other factors. Similar comments could be made about each of the thousands of stocks listed on the national stock exchanges, each of the hundreds of mutual funds, each of the thousands of U.S. and foreign coins available, antiques, stamps, or most other potential investments.

The real question is whether a specific item is a safe place in which to invest your money, and whether money can be made in the investment. My own definition of an investment is the turning over of some property or resource to another person or form, expecting a profit or an increase. We see this expectation from an investment in the parable of the talents. The man turned over some of his money to the three men, expecting to get his money back (safety of principal) and an increase in his investment (appreciation and/or interest).

Bear in mind there are no safe investments, except the treasures in heaven:

Do not lay up for yourselves treasures upon earth, where moth and rust destroy, and where thieves break in and steal. But lay up for yourselves treasures in heaven, where neither moth nor rust destroys, and where thieves do not break in or steal; for where your treasure is, there will your heart be also.
Matthew 6:19–21 NAS

Prerequisites To Financial Investments

Give at least a tithe to the Lord. "You must tithe all of your crops every year" (Deuteronomy 14:22 TLB). Don't expect God to bless your financial investments if you are robbing Him of the tithes which are rightfully His.

Pay off your debts. If you are investing money that rightfully is due others, then you really are investing money for others without their permission. The principle in the Scriptures is to pay your debts first, before investing your money. "Don't withhold repayment of your debts. Don't say 'some other time,' if you can pay now" (Proverbs 3:27, 28 TLB).

Commit your financial investments to God. Give up all your rights to your assets. Dedicate your investments to His glory, to be used for His purposes. He is trustworthy. While suffering in jail, Paul expressed his complete trust in Christ in this way: "For I know the one in whom I trust, and I am sure that he is able to safely guard all that I have given him until the day of his return" (2 Timothy 1:12 TLB). And He is the best investment manager of all.

Why Invest Money?

To plan ahead. "A sensible man watches for problems ahead and prepares to meet them. The simpleton never looks, and suffers the consequences" (Proverbs 27:12 TLB).

I am appalled at the number of Christians who violate this principle. I know several who have seen that their youngsters were in a church that preached the gospel. They have tried to provide a fine home (in most cases, even cars during high school) for their children. However, when the time came for the youngster to attend college, no money had been set aside to pay for an education in a private Christian school or even to provide funds to leave home and attend a public institution. In every case I know of, it was not because of a lack of income on the part of the parents. The irony is that if the income of the parents had been low enough, the youngster would have been able to secure a scholarship or tuition grant to help with college expenses. The parents had placed more emphasis on "things" during the formative years than on laying aside money to provide for college expenses when that time arrived.

To provide for your family in time of need. "But anyone who won't care for his own relatives when they need help, especially those living in his own family, has no right to say he is a Christian. Such a person is worse than the heathen" (1 Timothy 5:8 TLB).

I remember an example from years ago of a boy in our 10th-grade Sunday school class. His father, through sharing the Word of God with him, taught him about tithing. While working as a busboy in a local cafe during high school, this boy earned $150 monthly. Every month he knew the joy of giving. He sent $5 to his church, $5 to his needy grandfather in Florida, and $5 to the Billy Graham Evangelistic Association. (He had told me that the Billy Graham television programs were a real ministry in his life.) This young man already was following God's commandments to care for his own family.

Statistics reveal that most men do not save money. As a result, they reach the sunset years of life with little or no income. Look at the table below to discover the fortune that will be earned between the first and last pay checks.

Total Earnings to Age 65

Age	Average monthly income $ 2,000	$ 2,500
25	$960,000	$1,200,000
30	840,000	1,050,000
35	720,000	900,000
40	600,000	750,000
45	480,000	600,000
50	360,000	450,000
55	240,000	300,000

Since so many earn fortunes, you would think men in their preretirement years would accumulate substantial assets. The facts prove otherwise. One government study indicated that half of America's married men aged 58 to 63 had financial assets of no more than a few thousand dollars (excluding property equity).

Providing for your family in time of need means saving now. A prudent plan for managing your income so that a regular nest egg is built should provide money for unforeseen emergencies, retirement living and an inheritance for your children.

The enemy of the nest egg is procrastination. Note the excuses of those who always seem to put off saving money until later:

AGES 25–30:	I can't save now. I'm just getting started and my income is low.
AGES 30–40:	I can't save now. I have a young family to raise.
AGES 40–50:	I can't save now. I have two children in college.
AGES 50–60:	I can't save now. My wife and I want to enjoy life.
AGES 60–65:	I can't save enough between now and retirement time to make much difference.
AGES 65+:	I can't save now. I'm living with my son and his wife.

Mishandling our personal finances is grounds for disqualification for a church responsibility. Paul writes: "He must manage his own household well, keeping his children submissive and respectful in every way; for if a man does not know how to manage his own household, how can he care for God's church?" (1 Timothy 3:4, 5 RSV). The idea here is very clear. Mismanaging family finances disqualifies us for holding leadership positions in the church. No wonder many churches are in spiritual and financial trouble.

Investing our savings proves our faithfulness and provides for future contingencies, family emergencies, and inheritances for our children. God is pleased when we honor Him by saving and investing.

Investments Are Not Without Dangers

You may begin to trust in financial resources instead of trusting God. Proverbs clearly warns us: "Trust in your money and down you go! Trust in God and flourish as a tree!" (Proverbs 11:28 TLB). And "The rich man thinks of his wealth as an impregnable defense, a high wall of safety. What a dreamer!" (Proverbs 18:11 TLB).

You may become entangled with your investments. Some of the investor's time and energy usually is required for the monitoring of financial resources. Paul's warning in Timothy is clear: "And as Christ's soldier do not let yourself become tied up in worldly affairs, for then you cannot satisfy the one who has enlisted you in his army" (2 Timothy 2:4 TLB). Woe that I should not be able to satisfy Christ with my life because of a consuming interest in financial investments! "Don't weary yourself trying to get rich. Why waste your time? For riches can disappear as though they had the wings of a bird!" (Proverbs 23:4,5 TLB).

Your investments may lead you to increased temptations. Rapidly increasing assets may tempt you to personal pride. Or you may react to a sudden or extensive decrease in your assets with moodiness or depression. Paul covers these conditions precisely: "For men who set their hearts on being wealthy expose themselves to temptation. They fall into a trap and lay themselves open to all sorts of silly and wicked desires, which are quite capable of utterly ruining and destroying their souls. For loving money leads to all kinds of evil, and some men in the struggle to be rich have lost their faith and caused themselves agonies of mind" (1 Timothy 6:9, 10 PHILLIPS).

You may develop a desire to get money. Such desire usually renders a Christian useless. Jesus is concerned about the heart attitude of a person. No matter how much you have, if you have an overwhelming desire to get rich, then you are serving the god of money instead of our God. Jesus sums this up: "But all too quickly the attractions of this world and the delights of wealth, and the search for success and lure of nice things come in and crowd out God's message from their hearts, so that no crop is produced" (Mark 4:19 TLB).

Just as no financial investment is without some risk, the very process of saving money also carries a degree of spiritual risk. Scriptural warnings help us develop right attitudes toward investing.

My Investment Priorities

Here is a list of my own priorities for the placement of my savings:

1. *The business the Lord has entrusted to my management.* "Develop your business first before building your house" (Proverbs 24:27 TLB). A debt-free business has been our goal.

2. *Our own house.* Based on the same verse, our goal was to pay for the place where we practice Christian hospitality.

3. *Life insurance.* I've carried life insurance since I was married, to provide for my wife and two daughters in case of my death. I was convinced of this responsibility by this statement of Paul's: "If any one does not provide for his relatives, and especially for his own family, he has disowned the faith and is worse than an unbeliever" (1 Timothy 5:8 RSV).

Whole life insurance premiums are a form of savings, since they are funds we are not spending. Now that our daughters are through college and on their own, we keep the life insurance, as it would allow more generous giving for Marjean in the event of my death. It also provides for substantial gifts to the Lord's work after we both die.

4. *Some readily available funds, invested in financial institutions.* As a small businessman, I have a responsibility to my coworkers. When the business loses money, there have to be reserves to continue to pay the expenses. "For the laborer is worthy of his wages" (Luke 10:7 NAS).

5. *All the income I can invest tax-free.* My own company has a qualified profit-sharing trust. Each eligible employee (a full-time

employee with two years' service) and I receive, from company profits, about 15 percent of our annual salaries, tax-free, into the trust.

Do you know of any way to earn an investment return comparable to that of not paying income taxes on the top 15 percent of your salary? I don't!

For this reason, I usually recommend that people take advantage of company qualified savings and retirement plans. Of course, there is then the decision of whether the money is to be invested in a bank, savings and loan, credit union, life insurance company, mutual fund, or some other authorized investment medium. You'll have to seek further counsel for that specific decision.

6. *Common stocks.* Solomon gave us one of the Bible's soundest investment principles: "Steady plodding brings prosperity; hasty speculation brings poverty" (Proverbs 21:5 TLB). For the beginning investor, a family of well-managed mutual funds may be the answer. Regular monthly investments meet the steady plodding test.

7. *A reasonable amount of food, water, and emergency fuel is wise planning.* Strikes, revolution, wars, weather crises, and fuel shortages all can cause a disruption in the stocking of supermarket shelves, as well as our ability to store perishables at home. Some reasonable investment in such provisions could pay dividends in more ways than economic ones.

How Should You Invest Your Nest Eggs?

An understanding of the prerequisites of investment and a commitment to God's pattern for investing brings us to the question of how and where we should invest the nest eggs.

The old investment adage is: DON'T PUT ALL YOUR EGGS IN ONE BASKET. The city of Wichita, KS, would have done well to have followed that admonition when trees were planted along its streets. Someone decided the ideal tree for Wichita was the Dutch elm. Thousands of Dutch elms were planted throughout the city. As they grew, they lined the streets and provided shade in our neighborhoods, making our city among the most shaded in the nation. Suddenly, like a thief in the night, the Dutch elm disease came. There was no known preventive and no known cure. Up and down the streets were gaps as the trees died and were removed.

No matter what the eggs are, putting them all into one basket is a most hazardous way.

My idea of investments is to diversify according to these priorities: 1) life insurance, 2) business or profession, 3) house, 4) deferred compensation, and 5) other investments.

Life insurance is first because that's the only way I know for most of us to provide for our families in the event of our own deaths. Whether you buy term insurance or whole life insurance should depend on your own analysis of the costs and benefits of each kind. What is right for one person may be wrong for another.

Your business or profession should rank next as an investment. Your own education is an investment of time and money that should pay excellent returns during your working years.

If you decide to be in business for yourself, your own efforts will largely determine the success or failure of the business. There are millions of small businesses in operation, so you have plenty of successful examples to encourage you. You also must recognize the great risk in starting your own company; statistics show most new businesses will fail.

The principle of Scripture is to invest in your business, which will be productive, then build your house (Proverbs 24:27). Most people reverse this. The large house purchased early in life tends to involve so much of their money that investing in a business is out of the question.

If your work for a company, you may be involved in its pension or profit sharing plan. Funds are set aside for you now, without deductions for income taxes. If you are self-employed or work for a company that has no retirement plan, you may qualify for your own individual retirement account. It is possible to set up a savings account on which you pay no tax on the income saved now or on the annual interest earned by your savings. Taxable withdrawals are planned for retirement age in such a way that the potential tax savings may be significant. Consult a financial specialist for details.

Other areas of investment are almost as varied as the imagination can stretch. Real estate, oil, commodities, stocks, bonds, antiques, stamps, coins, jewelry, art, rare books, artifacts, guns, bottles, dolls, or virtually anything people collect can be considered investments. Some of these, such as stocks, bonds, and real estate, pay a return on an annual basis. Others are held with the expectation that they will increase in value as time goes by.

Your investments beyond life insurance, business, and home should be teamed with your own interests and personality. If you were raised on a farm and you have a knowledge of agricultural products, you understand the intricacies of weather and the price variables of feed and fertilizer, and you enjoy keeping abreast of the farm situation, then you might pursue a lifelong interest in agricultural investments. You could include everything from commodity purchases to owning and acquiring farm land. If common stocks are your interest, you might specialize in a study of those companies which are primarily agriculture-oriented. Or you might own a herd of cattle or hogs.

I chose to pursue the area of common stocks. By reading annual reports of companies in which I have invested, I am able to keep abreast of a cross-section of American business. Most annual reports share not only the past history but also the goals and objectives for the future. As a businessman, I find these interesting; they also give me vision and ideas for my own small business.

One friend of mine enjoyed working on old houses as a means of relaxation. He bought houses close to where he lived and fixed them up for renting. They provided work opportunities for his boys as they grew up. When the youngsters left home, the houses had appreciated in value. Since my friend's interests by then had changed, he sold the properties at a substantial gain.

Most of these investments we have discussed are the kind that lend themselves to systematic investing. The regular monthly payment on the home for a 20-year mortgage results in having a home completely paid for. Yearly whole life insurance premiums not only provide insurance in case of sudden death but also add up to retirement values. Steady hard work in your own business often results in a substantial salable asset. The key to investing in the stock market is to set aside regular amounts for systematic investment.

I never have been successful in knowing when the market was too high or too low. In fact, figures prove that most individual investors buy high and sell low. After all, it takes real courage to buy when the stock market is low, the news is bad, and the future looks bleak. That's the time most individuals sell out.

Setting aside money regularly to invest in the stock market means that when the market is down you will buy more shares with your money. When the market is up, you will buy fewer shares. By investing steadily, you are doing what is called *dollar cost averaging*. If you believe in the long-term financial future of America and the world, this is one way to express that belief.

An illustration of dollar cost averaging will reveal its principle and its power. Assume the price of a stock selling at $10 a share drops 50 percent—obviously a bad situation. Even worse, assume you had bought $100 worth at $10 per share — obviously bad timing.

But also assume you invested $100 at each point of change thereafter as the stock dropped all the way to $5 and then recovered to $10.

This is not a roaring bull market example—yet what happened overall was very satisfactory.

$100 Invested Each Point Down the Ladder & Each Point Back Up

Bought 10.000 shs. @ $10	$10 = 10.000 shs.
11.111 shs. @ $9	$9 = 11.111 shs.
12.500 shs. @ $8	$8 = 12.500 shs.
14.286 shs. @ $7	$7 = 14.286 shs.
16.667 shs. @ $6	$6 = 16.667 shs.
	$5 = 20.000 shs.

Total invested $1,100.00
Total shares bought = 149.128
End value (149.128 x $10) $1,491.28
Total gain = 35.6%

Remember, at no point did the stock ever sell above your initial price—but in the end you had a 35-percent profit. And this does not include whatever dividends the stock might have paid. This is the value of dollar cost averaging!

The previous table is, of course, hypothetical. An investor should realize no investment program can assure a profit or protect against loss in declining markets. The investor would incur a loss if he or she discontinued the program during a period when the market value of the share was less than what was paid for it. For this reason, any investor contemplating such a program should take into account his or her ability to continue it during any such period. However, the figures do provide comfort to those who assume what comes down will go back up.

Is it not also reasonable to assume what goes up may come back down? I wanted to see what the same illustration would reveal for the dollar averager who started buying shares when they were low, continued buying up to $10, and bought all the way back down to where the investor started. Here's the comparison:

$100 Invested Each Point Up the Ladder & Each Point Back Down

Bought 20.000 shs. @ $5	$5 = 20.000 shs.
16.667 shs. @ $6	$6 = 16.667 shs.
14.286 shs. @ $7	$7 = 14.286 shs.
12.500 shs. @ $8	$8 = 12.500 shs.
11.111 shs. @ $9	$9 = 11.111 shs.
	$10 = 10.000 shs.

Total invested	$1,100.00
Total shares bought = 149.128	
End value (149.128 x $5)	$ 745.64
Total loss = 32.2%	

Timing in any investment is crucial. If you invested steadily, as in the above illustration, and had to sell when the stock was back down to $5, you would have lost 32.2 percent of your investment. I have found no way to avoid risk in investments.

Don't get me wrong: I'm not knocking the steady-plodding principle in investments. But no method I know of *guarantees* a riskless investment. At the time you want or need to sell any holding, it may be worth more or less than you paid for it. The value will be determined entirely by what the buyer wants to pay you for the holding.

Of course, as a Christian, I realize everything we see will burn some day. "The day of the Lord is surely coming, as unexpectedly as a thief, and then the heavens will pass away with a terrible noise and the heavenly bodies will disappear in fire, and the earth and everything on it will be burned up" (2 Peter 3:10 TLB). But for now, I do live in this world, and I am called to be faithful in what God has given me.

We are warned in Scripture to avoid get-rich-quick investments. "The man who speculates is soon back to where he began — with nothing. This, as I said, is a very serious problem, for all his hard work has been for nothing; he has been working for the wind. It is all swept away. All the rest of his life he is under a cloud — gloomy, discouraged, frustrated, and angry" (Ecclesiastes 5:15–17 TLB). There is no way I could warn you more clearly against get-rich-quick schemes than the Bible has done. Yet, millions of dollars are lost each year to fraudulent deals because of the greed of investors.

The salesperson who pressures you to BUY NOW should trigger a red warning flag in your mind. Consider the "friend" who drops by to give you an opportunity to "invest" in a red-hot oil deal. Unfortunately, you must decide tonight because "they are going to start drilling in the morning."

There is an understandable reason for so many mistakes in financial matters by Christians. We know little about the complicated nature of life insurance and all of its variables, to say nothing of the hundreds of companies from which one may purchase insurance. If we go into a small business, we usually do it with no previous small business experience, at least from an owner's point of view. Even purchasing a home is an occasional experience for most people. Except for the professional investor, those who invest in anything certainly could be considered rank amateurs.

Most people make major financial expenditures without really looking at all the facts. Such action is downright dangerous and certainly not smart. "What a shame — yes, how stupid! — to decide before knowing the facts!" (Proverbs 18:13 TLB). The ultimate cost and alternative possibilities seldom are considered when someone is being swept along in a desire to acquire a new home, car, business, or investment. It usually is not comfortable to seek counsel, as most of us want to do what we want to do when we want to do it. It is possible that the counselor might suggest the step is not a good one for us. Then we are in the position of doing it anyway, in spite of the godly counsel we have sought. Or we have to give up our own desire, which is seldom easy.

Obtain Godly Counsel

One of the best investments I ever made has been a relationship. By the grace of God, I developed a relationship with a Christian financial planner. He has given me counsel in life insurance as well as other areas of my life. As a competent financial planner, he is aware of the trends in taxation, business, investments, wills, trusts, and profit sharing programs. His counsel in each area has been substantial. In addition, he performs an annual review of my financial situation. Through skillful questioning concerning my future goals, he has stimulated some significant analysis in several areas of my life.

What joy it is to pray regularly with my counselor, share in Christian service with him, and know that the financial counsel he provides comes out of a mutual love for me and a common fellowship with the Lord Jesus Christ. When I say this relationship has been an investment, I can say truthfully that it has taken effort to keep the relationship growing, but it has born fruit in both our lives.

Your most effective counselors will be those who know you best. Developing relationships with counselors who are competent in several areas can be an excellent investment. Godly counsel is a must for the Christian investor.

The hatching of your nest eggs should not be left to chance. For each egg to accomplish the greatest financial benefit, you must know what to expect when they hatch.

13: When the Eggs Hatch

A good egg hatches sooner or later. Your nest egg may be the source of many possibilities for your mature years. You will notice that retirement has not been mentioned.

Just as he was preparing to change from his full-time college professor status, Dr. Elton Trueblood said he was looking forward to retirement as a time to do those things for which he had prepared during his lifetime. During a speech to the annual meeting of the Wichita Chamber of Commerce, he asked this perceptive question: "Can you imagine retiring and moving away to Florida to play shuffleboard the rest of your life?" Sunny leisure was not Dr. Trueblood's idea for his mature years.

Your own plans for your later years may not be formulated. A preview of the potential income for your planned nest egg can be profitable in two ways:

1. For financial planning. A realistic view of your income possibilities may surprise you. They certainly have surprised me. Your income may be insufficient for you to cease all work for pay. Or your income may support you in such a way that your financial freedom will allow tremendous opportunities for Christian service.

2. For stimulating provocative questions about your future. "How can the Lord best use my gifts then?" "What can I do now to prepare for my ministry then?" "What would I do if I had the expected amount of income now and didn't need to do my present work to produce it?" "Do I need to make adjustments now in order to increase my expected income then?" You probably will have several questions of your own.

Depending on which nest eggs you have when you reach

retirement, you may have income from one or more of at least four sources: Social Security, life insurance, company retirement program, and personal investments.

SOCIAL SECURITY. The money deducted for your pay check for Social Security will return an income of, typically, several hundred dollars each month if you retire at age 62 or later. If your wife also is 62, she will receive an additional amount equal to half of your benefits.

Social Security changes have been frequent in the past. Changes will continue in the future. To figure your specific situation, a visit to the nearest Social Security Administration office is recommended. Materials are available to help you estimate your future benefits, based on the current benefit scales.

LIFE INSURANCE. The person who buys whole life insurance has several options upon retirement:

1. Hold a paid-up insurance policy. This means no further premiums are paid. When the insured dies, the amount of insurance is paid to the beneficiary.

2. Use the cash value of the policy to purchase an annuity. This guarantees a monthly income for life.

3. Take out the cash value and invest it yourself. When you cash in your policy, the difference between your cost and your value would be taxable income. The sum remaining after taxes either can be invested to yield income (which you can spend) or set up in a monthly withdrawal plan of principal and income for a predetermined number of years.

COMPANY PENSION PLAN. There are approximately as many varieties of company retirement programs as there are companies. Our purpose is to encourage you to look at your benefits now. What might you expect to receive in benefits when you retire?

A normal objective is for the worker's pension plan plus Social Security to produce 50 to 60 percent of the worker's normal earnings in retirement benefits. These pension benefits usually are taxable, except to the extent of the employee's own contributions to the plan.

PERSONAL INVESTMENTS. You may want to know how much money you will have upon retirement if you start now to invest a specific amount each month. A bank can provide tables showing you the growth of monthly deposits at selected rates of interest, compounded semi-annually. The following table shows some examples of the growth of planned savings.

Growth of Monthly Deposits (in Dollars)

5% INTEREST

Years	$1	$10	$25	$50	$100
1	$ 12.33	$ 123.27	$ 308.18	$ 616.36	$ 1,233
5	68.20	682.01	1,705.01	3,410.03	6,820
10	155.50	1,555.03	3,887.58	7,775.16	15,550
15	267.26	2,672.58	6,681.44	13,362.89	26,726
20	410.31	4,103.13	10,257.83	20,515.65	41,031

6% INTEREST

Years	$1	$10	$25	$50	$100
1	$ 12.39	$ 123.93	$ 309.83	$ 619.66	$ 1,239
5	69.99	699.87	1,749.67	3,499.35	6,999
10	164.04	1,640.44	4,101.09	8,202.18	16,404
15	290.45	2,904.48	7,261.20	14,522.40	29,045
20	460.32	4,603.25	11,508.12	23,016.23	46,032

To illustrate, suppose you planned to save $50 monthly for 20 years prior to age 65. At a five-percent semi-annual compound rate, you would have $20,515.65 at the end of that time. Each year your

$20,515.65 would earn approximately $1,026 in interest. You could withdraw approximately $85 each month while allowing your investment to remain intact. Or you might decide to withdraw your entire savings at age 65 and convert them to an annuity.

In today's economy, it should be obvious that the more you can save each month, the better off you'll be at retirement.

Value of $1 Invested

VARYING COMPOUND ANNUAL INTEREST RATES

Year	4%	5%	6%	8%
1	$1.04000	$1.05000	$1.06000	$1.08000
5	1.21665	1.27628	1.33822	1.46932
10	1.48024	1.62889	1.79084	2.15892
15	1.80093	2.07892	2.39654	3.17216
20	2.19111	2.65328	3.20712	4.66094
25	2.66582	3.38633	4.29184	6.84844
30	3.24337	4.32191	5.74345	10.06260

The above table can be useful for planning what a specific sum of money saved now will be worth at a later date. For instance, $1 drawing interest at six percent will be worth $2.39654 in 15 years; $1,000 will have a value of $2,396.54. You can estimate what funds set aside now will be worth later, when needed for college expenses or retirement.

The next table shows the amount you would have to deposit each month — in an account earning interest from day of deposit to day of withdrawal at 5.25 percent compounded daily — to accumulate the sum in the center column. The right side of the table gives the amount you could withdraw from the account each month until the funds are depleted.

Planned Savings & Withdrawals (in Dollars)

MONTHLY DEPOSITS (YEARS)					MONTHLY WITHDRAWALS (YEARS)			
5	10	15	20	Total	5	10	15	20
72.56	31.48	18.10	11.64	5,000	95.11	53.84	40.41	33.92
145.13	62.96	36.21	23.29	10,000	190.22	107.69	80.82	67.85
217.69	94.44	54.31	34.94	15,000	285.45	161.54	121.23	101.77
290.26	125.93	72.42	46.59	20,000	380.45	215.39	161.64	135.70
435.39	188.89	108.63	69.88	30,000	570.68	323.09	242.47	203.45
580.52	251.86	144.84	93.18	40,000	760.91	430.78	323.29	271.40
725.65	314.82	181.06	116.47	50,000	951.13	538.48	404.12	339.25

This table can be helpful in deciding how much you need to save monthly, now, so that specific sums can be accumulated. You also can learn how much those accumulated sums can produce in monthly withdrawals for a certain time period. For instance, you may estimate that college costs of $761 per month will be needed for a five-year period, with 10 years to save before this need arises. You must save approximately $252 each month to accumulate the $40,000 needed to provide $760.91 in monthly withdrawals for five years.

Consider your family life cycle. If child bearing, rearing, and "launching" take the first 25 years of a marriage, the married couple may be 50 years old by the time the children are "launched" and on their own. With some planning, the couple could have paid off a 20-year home mortgage by the time their nest is empty. By continuing to invest for 15 more years that portion of the house payment which applied to interest and principal, their nest egg for age 65 could be substantial.

Where will *you* be in regard to income when your eggs hatch? Completion of a monthly retirement income estimate form *now* could save many surprises later. God continually warns us not to *depend* on annuities, Social Security, or dividends for our future. "We can make our plans, but the final outcome is in God's hands" (Proverbs 16:1 TLB).

DON'T FORGET WHO IS YOUR CHIEF INVESTMENT COUNSELOR!

14: What About Those Scriptural Contradictions?

Two verses seem to indicate the Bible says it is wrong to save. "For we walk by faith, not by sight" (2 Corinthians 5:7 RSV). "Lay not up for yourselves treasures upon the earth. . . ." (Matthew 6:19 KJV).

Many people think any financial saving shows a lack of faith in God's provision. Many also feel that any savings beyond current expenses is laying up treasures upon earth. These people conclude that saving and investing violate Scripture.

Scripture also teaches the savings principle (see Proverbs 21:20; 22:3). Admittedly, there are some tensions in the Bible:

- We are to work — and to rest.
- We are to save — and to live by faith.
- We are to give — and to spend.

The focus is to be on God, God's things, God's ways. Our aim must not be primarily on money or how we are spending it. We should want to use our lives and our resources to serve the Lord Jesus Christ. You may have noticed that the Bible has more to say about the dangers of money than about the blessings of money.

The biblical principle is for us to be savers. But we are not to store money. There's a real difference between saving and storing money. One way to test your own savings is to ask yourself whether you would refuse to meet real needs from your savings. If so, you're laying up treasures and not really saving. The mark of a saver is generosity. The storer won't be a generous person, since there will always be a reason to store money.

Does the use of your money reflect that you live for eternity or for yourself and for now? Your check stubs will answer your own question. The Bible says, "Love not the world, neither the things that are in the world. If any man love the world, the love of the Father is not in him" (1 John 2:15 KJV).

The real key is balance — balance between giving, saving, and spending; balance between work and rest; balance between family and ministry.

Marjean's 2¢: Savings

George already has talked about the fact that a storer won't be a generous person. In a budget workshop, my friend Lynn and I were asked what a mother should do about a child who refused to spend his money, but just saved it. Lynn answered by saying she had one like that. What she had discovered, though, was that the child wouldn't spend *his* money but was willing to spend *someone else's* — that is, his parents'. I'd say he was a storer. A child needs to be taught to spend properly.

What was my part in helping in this training of our daughters? First of all, I was to "fit into my husband's plans" (see 1 Peter 3:1). I was to support his plan of training. If I gave my daughter a nickel or a dime or a dollar, then I was saying, in effect, "Come to me if you run out of money." I was undermining all that her father was trying to teach her.

Oh, how easy it would have been to give in. Amy and I had spent hours, it seemed, at the shopping center looking for a certain kind of shoes she wanted (she had her own clothing allowance). Finally we found the shoes. She tried on her size, then asked the price. Quietly she said to me, "That's too much! I don't have that much in my budget."

I was tired. It was late in the day. Supper needed fixing. I wanted to say, "Oh, honey, I'll give you the difference. Just get them."

But fortunately, God revealed to me that I was to be my husband's helpmeet, a helper fit for him. I would be of no help to George or to Amy if I gave in. Consistency and example are two good teachers.

Is it any wonder that both our girls have become excellent

shoppers and managers of their money?

You may ask, as others have: What about the child's savings? Did you just let them build up?

Yes, we let them build up and put the coins into a savings bank that registered the amount. Then we, along with the child, took the bank to the savings and loan company, where it was opened and the money deposited in our daughter's name. This is a good opportunity to teach your children about putting their money to work for them.

I would suggest that if the child wants to purchase a big item, allow the child to use some of his or her own money for it. I remember Jenny, our oldest, taking her money out to buy her dog. This was the deal her father made with her when she was 6 years old. She could have a dog if she saved for it. He helped her with the purchase, but that puppy was very important to her as she handed over her saved coins. (But I'm afraid we didn't go far enough in teaching her the purchase price was only the beginning of pet ownership.)

15: Two Ways To Give After You Live

One-to-one is the statistic. The ratio has never changed. For every birth, there is a death!

Depending on how long you live, you may reap the results of the careful planning of your nest eggs. You also may take steps *now* that will enable others to harvest the fruits of your provision after the time of your death. These steps involve your body organs and your earthly possessions.

Body Organs

I once attended the funeral of a Christian brother. Although my friend had not been a prominent civic worker or a top corporation executive, the large downtown church was full for his funeral. As I thought about my relationship with this man, I realized he possessed some unusual giving qualities. His granddaughter had been born almost totally blind. Shortly after her birth, her parents had divorced. To fulfill his scriptural responsibilities, this grandfather began caring for the young girl. I have vivid memories of his bringing her to church, walking hand in hand with her, and fulfilling the responsibilities of parent to the girl. Whether assisting in the kindergarten or singing in the church choir, this fellow was always around, giving himself to little details that others simply were not interested in handling. In my opinion, his servant attitude revealed his giving spirit.

When the minister delivered the eulogy, I was struck with the thought of how my friend gave *after* he lived as well as *while* he lived. For within a couple hours after his death, his eyes were on the way

131

to the Kansas Eye Bank. His hope was that they could be useful to someone who had no vision.

While he lived, this man had taken the trouble to arrange for the gift of his eyes, with the expectation that someone else could see through them after he no longer needed those eyes. That action caused my wife and me to do some thinking about the stewardship of our own bodies at the time of our going to be with the Lord.

There are at least 17 transplantable organs. It is now possible to replace a variety of malfunctioning human organs, with increasing success.

Although I was challenged to consider this organ donation idea, for a long time I was probably like most of you reading this book. I simply did nothing about it. Had I died during that time, all my organs probably would be resting now in a casket beneath a few feet of dirt. However, while I wrote this chapter, I discussed the idea with Marjean. In the presence of two witnesses, we completed the anatomical gift section on the backs of our driver's licenses.

The provision to give your organs after you die is a very specific way to give after you live. Another specific way concerns your will.

Your Will

Do *you* have a will? If not, don't be too surprised to discover you are among the majority of adults in the United States who have no will.

Why is a will that important? What will happen to your property if you die without a will?

The answers to those questions will depend on state laws specifying how your property is to be distributed. It usually will be divided in some way among the next of kin, but probably not the way you would have liked to have had it divided. Because the court will appoint an administrator to distribute the property, there may be extra court expenses involved for the beneficiaries of your property. If there are no relatives, your property goes to the state.

Without a will, all of your property will be divided among relatives. None can be directed to any other beneficiary, such as to a church or charity. Not having a will is one way to make certain you do not give after you live.

You may say, "I'm too young to have a will," or "I have so little, why should I have a will?"

Right after my second child was born, my insurance agent talked to me about additional life insurance. He also asked if I had a will. I told him of course not, since I had hardly any property.

Then he asked me another question, "If you and your wife are killed in some kind of accident, who will raise your children?" Since I couldn't answer him, I just shrugged my shoulders and gave him a silly look.

That evening I talked to Marjean about that situation. Would we want my parents or hers to be responsible for raising the children? Would we want her brother and sister-in-law, newly married, to take over that responsibility, or would we choose one of our friends?

These were tough questions, and we really hated to grapple with them. After all, weren't the chances of our being killed in a common situation very, very slim?

But we couldn't dodge the issue. The chances were slight, but there was always that possibility. Also, we knew deep within our hearts that *we* wanted to dictate the guardianship of our children in case of a common disaster. We knew we were in the best position to make that decision. And we knew that if we were killed without having made a guardianship decision, someone else would make it.

It was this motivation, along with the urging of our insurance representative and a recognition that this was the businesslike step to take, that motivated us to prepare our first will.

Maybe you do have a will. Does it provide for any giving out of your estate?

If it does not, again, you need not be surprised. My own experience is that most wills do not go beyond the almost automatic passing-it-on-to-closest-relatives stance. Even among large givers, few Christians give thought to other ways they can plan their estates and contribute significantly to the cause of Jesus Christ, both now and in the years to come.

Preparing a will helped me make some long-range plans and forced me to make some decisions about my basic giving philosophy. It also compelled me to take a good hard look at my own financial assets as well as my responsibilities.

My accountant showed me how to save significant amounts of taxes through increased giving from my estate. I established trusts to cover three possibilities for my family: my death and my wife surviving, my death without my wife surviving, and my death with none of my family surviving. Under each circumstance, the trusts provided for gifts to specific Christian organizations after the purpose of the trusts had been served. In other words, the federal government actually encouraged me to give. If I took no steps, the federal government received the taxes. If I took the legal steps allowed under the law, then I could determine which of the works of Christ would benefit from a portion of my estate, and estate taxes could be saved.

I can't begin to tell you the joy I experienced when I finally felt I had my affairs and those of my wife in order through the creation of wills and trusts to meet our responsibilities and our desires after death. But don't let me mislead you. People postpone doing wills because procrastination is the easy thing to do. Most people simply never get to their wills.

Creating a standard will is, of course, easier than choosing specifically those organizations which will receive portions of what you elect to give. Preparing a thoughtful will which incorporated our giving philosophy was a difficult task, and it will be difficult for you, too. But again, let me encourage you to take these steps so you can choose *now* how you want to give after you live.

You may not have a Christian lawyer, or your Christian lawyer may have little experience in guiding you to effective giving. Nevertheless, there are places where you can receive help.

The chances are that you already have in mind one or two organizations which will be the recipients of your estate giving. Could it be the particular denomination of your church? Is there some other Christian organization that has had a significant ministry in your life or in the lives of your family?

Most Christian organizations have a stewardship department with professionally trained consultants to help you approach financial and estate planning on a spiritual level. These services usually are offered to you as a guide to stimulate your thinking. They are confidentially done without charge or obligation. Usually, the organizations make it clear they are not engaged in rendering legal or tax advisory service. They may point out the need for an attorney in your own state, since state laws govern wills, trusts and charitable gifts made in a contractual agreement. Representatives of these organizations can be very helpful to you, because they have vast experience with other Christians who desire to give after they live.

In preparing my will, I discovered that in the ordinary will it can be very difficult to allow the kind of flexibility desired. A trust agreement or other legal device may make sense in certain situations.

You will discover as you begin thinking through your own situation that there are many difficult questions to answer. It makes a lot of sense to grapple with those questions now and arrive at a desirable agreement, rather than wait until you are faced with a terminal illness, or leave such decisions to your mate to make after a sudden death.

I once visited a Christian, a businessman of some means, to discuss his will. I asked him if he had made any provision in his will for giving to the Lord's work after his death. He said no, and then asked, "Since I tithe now on all my income, haven't I fulfilled my obligation to the Lord?" My answer was that it's not a matter of obligation but of another giving opportunity. The Bible says we should give "not grudgingly, or of necessity, for God loveth a cheerful giver" (2 Corinthians 9:7 KJV).

Unfortunately, preparing a will is not as easy as picking up the telephone, dialing your attorney, and saying, "Prepare a will for me." Your lawyer can do that, but without facts and figures, the will would not end up being a very personal document for you. Even if you already have a will, it may not accomplish your present objectives. The entire purpose of a will is to accomplish the desires of the maker.

To aid you in gathering information for your will, make a personal fact-finding survey of your financial affairs. The preparation of this survey will have two advantages for you: 1) It will force you to gather some information and make some decisions concerning the planning of your financial affairs, and 2) it will provide the information necessary for you and your advisors to determine the most effective way to dispose of your property at the time of your death.

Making an effective will is not easy. But as Christians, who wants the easy way? Serving the Lord often means taking the harder path. It is certainly the desire of my life that I live to the glory of God.

Paul tells us: "Be sure that everything is done properly in a good and orderly way" (1 Corinthians 14:40 TLB). Having a will that includes the stewardship of my possessions after I no longer need them is one way I can give glory to God after I live and present a witness to others.

16: But God!

For several years after I became a Christian, I tried to give more money to the Lord. I can't tell you what a relief it was when I finally took the plunge and decided to give a tenth of my gross income to the Lord's work.

My wife and I had been in a home Bible study group for several months. One night the thrust of the discussion centered around trusting versus trying. There seems to be a fine line between trying so hard to do something and trusting the Lord to do it for you. We knew we wanted to trust the Lord for every area of our lives. There was a gnawing suspicion that trying to give Him a little more money each year was not really trusting Him to meet all of our needs. Somehow I was directed by the Scriptures that if I was unwilling to give God at least 10 percent of my total income, then I really was not trusting Him at all. Proverbs 3:4-6 has been a great help in this area. The Living Bible says, "If you want favor with both God and man, and a reputation for good judgment and common sense, then trust the Lord completely; don't ever trust yourself. In everything you do, put God first, and he will direct you and crown your efforts with success." It has been exciting to trust Him more and more, and the percentage of our income that is given to the Lord's work has increased in proportion to our trust in Him.

Because I am so practical, I developed a very unscriptural habit of giving. From time to time preachers had told me in sermons that a person was to give in proportion as he received his income. This seemed like a ridiculous waste of checks, time, and energy, to me. Consequently, I made my pledge and with one grand swoop sent a check for all of it at the end of the year. Such action gave me the added security that if I had had a bad year, then I might just postpone payment of my pledge until the next year. During those days I also was considering whether I needed the tax deduction more in the

137

current year or whether I should postpone the gift until the first of the new year in order to have the deduction mean the most to me. There also was the element of pride involved, since I reasoned that not everyone in the church would have the kind of discipline I had and be able to plunk down an entire church pledge in one fell swoop.

But God!

But God zapped me with His Word again. "On every Lord's Day each of you should put aside something from what you have earned during the week, and use it for this offering. The amount depends on how much the Lord has helped you earn. Don't wait until I get there and then try to collect it all at once" (1 Corinthians 16:2 TLB). God's Word made it clear that I was to give regularly in proportion to my income.

The practical application of this lesson was to establish a separate bank account for our giving. Each pay day, our giving amount automatically is set aside from our income and deposited into the *giving account*. Checks are specially printed in a different color from our usual spending checks. We even have the fish symbol on the checks as a witness to all who receive them. Whenever extra income arrives, the giving percentage is set aside in the giving account.

Giving God the first part of all my income is a specific way I can put Him first in my life. "The purpose of tithing is to teach you always to put God first in your lives" (see Deuteronomy 14:23). One of my friends says tithing *was not instituted by God to raise money* but to train children.

Have you experienced the joy that comes from taking that initial step of establishing the tithe as a regular reminder that it all belongs to God?

Consider another advantage of the separate giving account. Most taxpayers do not claim charitable contributions at the level of anything like 10 percent or more of their gross income. In talking to other tithers, I have found that most of them have had their tax returns audited by the Internal Revenue Service. In each case, the primary focus of the audit was on the charitable contributions.

My own mother, who is a tither, was summoned recently by the Internal Revenue Service to produce evidence of her charitable contributions. I had the same experience a few months later. The separate checkbook made our audits a pleasant experience.

The discovery that there can be more to giving than simply sending a check has been a real blessing to us. A young man and his wife once stopped by our house en route to their new campus ministry at a state university. We had heard the young man's testimony a few months earlier. When given the opportunity, we were delighted to have a financial part in their ministry. When he explained their financial needs, he said his support already had reached a level of so many hundred dollars per month. Then he shared his goal with us. Our response was to tell him we would like to be involved for a specific amount each month. After we had prayer with them and they left, my wife and I agreed we also should send some words of encouragement with our monthly check.

Since that time, we have developed a personal involvement with the couple. They have stayed in our home several times, and we have shared the hospitality of their home. Seldom has a month gone by in which we have not communicated with each other by letter or telephone. Whenever we have a special prayer request, we advise them of it, knowing they will pray faithfully. The blessings we have received have far exceeded the small monthly gift we have given.

My business is to try to collect bills people did not pay to their creditors. A collection agency is really in the salvage business. When a creditor gives up trying to collect his own accounts, he turns them over to a collection agency. Our job is to locate the people who owe the money and sell them on the idea of paying the bill. We essentially are issuing calls to responsibility. I feel that people should keep the promises they make to other people about money. Otherwise, they lose some self-respect and carry around a load of guilt.

Some years ago, a military credit union sent us an account to collect in the amount of $285. The airman who owed the note had been discharged from the Air Force for car theft and for being AWOL. His whereabouts were unknown. For several months one of my employees followed his trail all over the United States. The car on which the money was owed was sold, and the young man was involved in drugs.

But God!

But God got hold of this fellow through a friend. We located him in a Teen Challenge center in Texas. The director of the center told us the former airman was there in his first few weeks as a Christian.

He was in the process of withdrawing from drugs and was beginning a study of God's Word. The director explained very carefully that the new convert had no money, was receiving no income, and would not be able to work for several months.

Imagine our surprise a few weeks later when we received a letter from the debtor along with a check for $135. His letter said, "The Lord has provided this money to pay on my debt. As soon as He provides more, I will send it."

I don't know what kind of image you have of a bill collector or what kind of experience you may have had with one. But the collector in my office who received this letter excitedly shared it with me. Could it be that God had changed the direction of this young man's life? We remembered, "If anyone is in Christ, he is a new creation." How could we be an encouragement to him? We sent his receipt and a contribution to Teen Challenge. We wrote a note of encouragement to the fellow for facing the responsibility of paying his debt.

Within a few days he wrote to our office. Thus began a regular correspondence between him and our own family. It was a thrill to watch him grow in Christ. He graduated from two Teen Challenge programs. His debt to the credit union was completely paid, as well as other debts he made during his wild sprees. He enrolled in a Bible college, training to be a full-time worker with Teen Challenge.

The first Christmas after we corresponded with him, we had the pleasure of having him in our home for a few days. Through a simple act of giving, God built a meaningful relationship and Christian fellowship that will extend into eternity.

Do you see what I mean about fantastic opportunities for giving?

More Than Money Goes Into Giving

People frequently ask whether all my giving is done through my local church. In my case, the answer to that is no. Approximately 50 percent of my giving supports ministries beyond the local church. We enjoy supporting individuals who have ministries in which we can be involved.

For each of these individual ministries, we have a small card. Each morning at our breakfast table we pray for the person on the top card of the group. We pray for the person's family and ministry. A large world map next to our breakfast table enables us to use pins for visual evidence of where these ministries are taking place. As we give, we feel a responsibility to pray for those with whom we are involved.

One of the great discoveries of my life was a "spiritual vacation." For years I had flown a small airplane all over the United States so that my family might enjoy the tourist attractions of this great country. Most of the time we arrived back home exhausted and broke. I usually called these trips *vacation* because I heard once that "a vacation is what you take when you can't take what you're taking any longer." But I hardly felt renewed spiritually or restored physically.

But God!

But God led us to a summer conference at The Navigators' headquarters in Colorado Springs, CO. If you have not experienced the true refreshment that comes from a week in Christian fellowship, Bible study, and prayer, you will not understand what I am talking about. Since our first taste of a spiritual vacation, we have not had a year when we did not return to some kind of Christian learning experience for a deeper feeding from God's Word.

Such spiritual vacations may be a legitimate income tax deduction. Since I am not qualified to provide tax counsel, I suggest you check with your tax advisor before claiming a deduction for any trip.

Many trips have been training experiences for my wife and me, and our training then has been used in service to our local church congregation. My CPA has advised me that the use of such training usually qualifies a trip for a tax deduction. The Internal Revenue Service agreed with me on my last audit. (But don't forget to keep good records.)

Giving beyond the tithe has been a joy for us. Have you experienced this joy in your own life, or are you holding out on God and trusting in your money? *Your checkbook will indicate whether you are really trusting God or trusting your money.*

The Prophet Malachi clearly shows that there is a difference in our lives according to the way we rob God or give to Him:

"Will a man rob God? Surely not! And yet you have robbed me.

" 'What do you mean? When did we ever rob you?'

"You have robbed me of the tithes and offerings due to me. And so the awesome curse of God is cursing you, for your whole nation has been robbing me. Bring all the tithes into the storehouse so that there will be food enough in my Temple; if you do, I will open up the windows of heaven for you and pour out a blessing so great you won't have room enough to take it in! Try it! Let me prove it to you!"
Malachi 3:8–10 TLB

This is the Lord's message to the people of Israel, given through the prophet. God seems to be saying about generous and joyful giving: TRY IT — YOU'LL LIKE IT!

17: Victory Over the Squeeze

Money was involved in the best deal I ever made.

In the summer of 1949 I decided to hitchhike from Dallas, where I was attending college, back to my hometown in Kansas. Hitchhiking was a money-saving method of transportation. A friend took me up to the north edge of Dallas, and I started out from there. The first ride took me only to Denton, TX. As I got out of the car, a real Texas summer thunderstorm hit, and I hurriedly took shelter for a couple of hours.

After the storm cleared, I headed for the north end of town, where I held out my thumb again. The first car that stopped was a Model A Ford. Since I obviously was trying to get a ride, I couldn't figure out any way to tell the man I didn't want to get into his old car. Reluctantly, I climbed inside.

To this day, I still have a vivid memory of that scene. We were driving down the road with the wind roaring in all the openings of that ancient black auto. Next to me sat a large man with a black beard, dressed in a black suit. On the seat beside us was a thick, black Bible. I don't remember any of the conversation that day except one question the fellow shouted at me over the noise of the car: "Brother, are you a Christian?"

Confidently, I answered, "I sure am." I explained further, "I've gone to Sunday school and church all my life. I'm attending a Christian college, and I'm rooming with a young man who's studying to be a preacher." After all that, surely the old man believed I was a Christian. At least, if he didn't, I did!

Twelve years later, one of the ministers in the church where I belonged asked if my wife and I would accept a scholarship to attend a weeklong retreat in another city. By this time, I had been president of a Sunday school class, held several positions in the church, and even assisted my wife in teaching Sunday school. Attending a retreat

143

had never occurred to me. However, the minister said some scholarship money was available, and our way would be paid. Oh, how money does talk. The idea of going away to spend a week on a beautiful college campus — at someone else's expense — appealed to me.

While attending this retreat, my wife and I noticed the others there seemed to have a different spirit than we had experienced in church. They had a love for each other which was expressed openly, in various ways. They carried their Bibles around and were not only reading them, but apparently were excited about what they read.

During the week, we met in small prayer groups, and I experienced moments of prayer such as I never had known. Each morning began with a period of silence, in which the 150 participants sat under the cottonwood trees reading their Bibles. At the end of the 45 minutes, people began to stand up and indicate "what the Lord told them" as they had read their Bibles that morning. I had been reading my Bible, too, but I was dumbfounded to hear that God actually had spoken to others as they read. Such certainly was not my experience.

Sometime during the week, the old man's question came back to me. It was the first time I had thought about it since he had asked it 12 years earlier. The question kept echoing: "Brother, are you a Christian?" The answer was clear. Now I knew that sitting in church would not make me a Christian any more than spending all my time in a chicken house would make me a chicken. I was hungry to come into a loving, personal relationship with Jesus Christ.

During the final night of the retreat, the minister preached on this text from Revelation: "Behold, I stand at the door and knock; if any one hears my voice and opens the door, I will come in to him and eat with him, and he with me" (3:20 RSV). The minister explained the picture that hung in the front of the sanctuary — a painting of Jesus standing and knocking at a door. The door represented the heart of a person. There was no latch on the outside of the door. He said Jesus was a gentleman and would not force Himself into anyone's life. He further explained that Christ came into a life when the person on the inside opened the door and invited Him in.

The minister issued an invitation to anyone who had heard the Lord Jesus Christ knocking on the door of his heart and wanted to ask Him to come in. As he invited those to come forward who wanted to make that decision, I stood up. At the same moment Marjean stood and took my hand. Together we walked down the aisle, but individually we invited Christ to come into our lives.

As we returned home from that retreat, we talked about various areas of our lives. Once again, money reared its head. We had not driven many miles before I confessed to my wife the selfish attitude I had had concerning the college scholarship given to me by my national church organization which I had not yet chosen to repay. Previously, it had been sufficient for me to rationalize that, after all, it was a scholarship earned because of my superior high school grades. The national church organization had sent letters reminding me that the scholarship did not carry a legal obligation, but it did carry a moral agreement to repay. Those letters usually motivated me to an annual contribution of some $25 — which wouldn't even cover the interest on the $1,600 that had been furnished for my college education.

But God spoke clearly to me as a new Christian. On that trip home, we resolved to pay back every dollar of the scholarship so that other youngsters could have the same opportunity I'd had.

Our giving did increase substantially during the years immediately after we became Christians. It was not until I began a regular study and meditation on God's Word, however, that I was led to the position to tithe as well as give additional offerings. The joy of giving is a real blessing to us now.

Another blessing was the sharing of our giving with our two daughters. It was a delight to train them in giving as well as in the area of stewardship of their time and possessions. The Bible says, "Train up a child in the way he should go" (Proverbs 22:6 RSV). I believe part of that training includes faithfulness in whatever money the child has.

The Greatest Joy: Knowing Christ

You can see that money was involved in the best deal I ever made. Nothing I know compares with the joy of knowing Jesus Christ personally. Nothing I know compares with the privilege of sharing the first minutes of each day with Him. Nothing I know equals the excitement and amazement that comes from the super ways He answers my prayers. Nothing I know compares with the uncanny way God has of zapping me with His Word in my areas of weakness. Nothing I know compares with the thrill of my obedience to His commandments. When He says, "This is the way, walk ye in it" (Isaiah 30:21 KJV), and I do it, there is a peace and joy that transcends anything money can ever buy.

How about you? Have you made the best deal of your life? Have you invited the Lord Jesus Christ to come into your heart forever?

To experience the security of His Eternal Presence, why not close your eyes wherever you are now and invite Christ to come into your life? You can repeat this simple prayer:

> Lord Jesus, I acknowledge that I have heard You knocking at the door of my heart. I now invite You to come into my life. Thank You for being so patient with me, and thank You for giving me the gift right now of eternal life with You. Amen.

Welcome to God's forever family! You are now one of all God's children, and if money has been talking to you the way it did to me, you probably have some things to set in order with what God has allowed you to have.

If you were already a Christian and have read through this book, it is my prayer that God has given you some new insights and practical aids so you can become less faithful to unrighteous mammon and receive increased responsibilities in the true riches.

Are there portions of your financial life that need correction? Don't put it off. Those areas in which you are holding back are cancers. Conversely, in every area in which you are obedient, you can expect greater and greater blessings. Revelation 22:11 is a tremendous challenge for each of us, not only in areas of financial responsibility, but also in every area of our lives. The Living Bible states it this way: "And when that time comes, all doing wrong will do it more and more; the vile will become more vile; good men will be better; those who are holy will continue on in greater holiness."

The goal for our money as well as for every area of our lives is to continue on in greater holiness. To continue in holiness, we must continue in His Word. As Jesus said, "If you continue in my word, you are truly my disciples, and you will know the truth, and the truth will make you free" (John 8:31, 32 RSV).

I've discovered that Jesus is "the Way, and the Truth, and the Life" just as He said (John 14:6). I've also discovered that the Scriptures are the best financial handbook I've ever found.

You Can Have the Victory

One evening while I was working on this book, the phone rang. My friend John excitedly blurted out that his income tax refund had just arrived and the check totaled $500 more than his tax return had listed.

"Best of all," John said, "the amount is just enough to make the last payment on all my debts. I'll be *financially free!*"

John deserved to shout. Four years earlier, as a brand-new Christian, he'd sat on my couch. He'd owed $17,000 and owned some clothes, golf clubs, and a TV set. He had been working long hours each week at a low-paying job, while interest on the debt had kept it growing like spring dandelions.

During the past few years, many have called and written to share the thrill and rejoicing they experienced as they became financially free. Some quotes of theirs may encourage you in your struggle to become UNSQUEEZED.

FROM A COLLEGE PROFESSOR: "When you were here, we owed $1,400 on MasterCard and Visa — and it was getting higher. In our seven years of married life, it was the first time we had 'lost control' of any area of our finances. We needed your *warning*. And we heeded your advice. We had 'plastic surgery.' As of today we owe MasterCard and Visa *nothing*! We arc rejoicing.

"Also, we moved our giving above the 10-percent mark for the first time. True, it's only gone to 13 percent, but I'm really excited about the small gain."

FROM A YOUNG PASTOR: "God has used you to motivate us to commit our lives and finances to Him in a fuller and more complete way. Every time I fail to follow the principles I learned from you, God convicts me and brings me back into obedience."

***FROM A YOUNG MARRIED MAN WITH THREE CHIL-
DREN***: "When I first started your class, I quickly became aware just
how deeply in debt I was. It was a shock! After making a budget
outline, I found out that I wasn't making enough to pay the bills each
month. Gradually I was going deeper in debt.

"After having a private session with you, I received ideas that
would help me on my way to becoming financially free: ideas like
cutting back from three telephones to one; cutting back from two cars
to one; also, keeping a budget! But the best idea that I received from
the class was to do it through the Lord Jesus Christ. And I'm glad to
report it sure has helped.

"You told us to set a goal for the amount of time we needed to
get out of debt. My goal was one year. I was in debt $7,000, to start.
As of today I'm still $2,000 in debt. To a certain extent I have
succeeded in cutting it back quite a bit, but I also failed, because I
know if I had disciplined myself better and kept my budget going at
all times, I would have succeeded completely. I learned a good lesson.

"But I'm not discouraged. I know that, being patient and
dedicated, I will be financially free of debt. Thank you both, George
and Marjean, for your help and your financial class. And best of all,
thank the *Lord Jesus Christ*!"

What these people had in common was putting into practice in
their lives instructions from God's Word: "But be doers of the word,
and not hearers only, deceiving yourselves" (James 1:22 RSV). They
had become doers of the Word. In each case, they had decided to obey
God's Word by:

- Purposing to live within their incomes and avoiding new
debts.
- Setting up and following a financial budget.
- Facing the facts about cars and houses.
- Trusting God by giving Him the first 10 percent of all their
incomes.

Everyone we have counseled who has chosen to obey these

principles in Scripture has experienced a special blessing in facing the financial squeeze. That blessing, of course, comes as no surprise to me, since God promises to bless those who act on His Word: "But he who looks into the perfect law, the law of liberty, and perseveres, being no hearer that forgets but a doer that acts, he shall be blessed in his doing" (James 1:25 RSV).

How about you? Are you afraid of the squeeze? Are you caught in the squeeze? Ask God to bring to your mind what you know He says about money management — about saving, spending, debt, giving, keeping records, and getting the facts.

Now, begin — a step at a time — to obey His principles. You'll experience God's personal blessings in your life, and you'll begin to be a shining light for Jesus Christ, as you have victory over the financial squeeze, to His glory.

Questions & Answers

1. Is there a time in your early life when you will be more in debt?
My experience is that debt becomes a habit. The choice is between
debt and no debt. Once the line is crossed from no debt to debt, people
seldom pay off their charge accounts. The minute the car is paid off,
the question is, "What can we buy with those payments we've been
making?"

A friend of mine was given a bottle of champagne for his
wedding. With it came a card that read, "Don't open this until you
are out of debt." My friend laughingly told me that after 15 years of
marriage, the champagne was still unopened.

**2. How can a person in a low income bracket with two or three
children provide the necessities of living without going into debt?**
The question includes part of the answer. With or without debt,
persons of very low incomes probably will provide only the *necessities* of living and not the *niceties* of living. To borrow to provide
such necessities only means less money in the future, when payments
and interest come due.

**3. Would a debt-free population cause an economic depression in
the country?** Most certainly! If our government quit overspending
its income by the average $54 billion it has gone into debt during each
of the last three years, the economy would certainly suffer. And if
consumers began to pay off the $256 billion in consumer debt, while
not adding the 1978 increase of $40 billion, the economic ripples
would be felt throughout the world. But don't hold your breath! It's
almost like saying, "If every Christian tithed. . . ."

150

4. *What do you think about the national debt?* I think that, corporately, we're violating biblical principles. Someday we'll reap what we've sown for our greed. "So each of us shall give account of himself to God" (Romans 14:12 RSV).

5. *Do you recommend debt consolidation loans to pay off your bills, if you also change your spending habits?* I do not recommend borrowing as a way of getting out of debt. You just can't borrow your way out of debt. Transferring debt from higher interest to lower interest may make sense. If a person owed several accounts charging 18-percent interest, I've seen cases in which borrowing from his credit union at 12 percent to pay off the 18-percent accounts made sense. Most credit unions maintain insurance which pays off the credit union loan in case the borrower dies or becomes disabled.

6. *Aren't you overlooking two factors in counseling people to keep out of debt? By being in debt but paying regularly, I keep a good credit rating, in case of emergencies. In addition, the interest I pay really costs a lot less, since it is deductible from my income tax.* I prefer to be prepared for emergencies with savings rather than credit. Does the Bible glorify the ant (Proverbs 30:24, 25) because it has good credit? No! The ant stores up food for the winter. The ant is a saver.

As for those tax deductions, I prefer to list giving deductions rather than interest deductions. If Marjean and I had paid interest on our cars and major purchases throughout our years of marriage, our giving to the Lord's work would have been thousands of dollars less.

ON CREDIT CARDS

1. *Is it wrong to use credit cards?* I hope not, since I carry many of them when I travel. There's a big difference between using a credit card for *credit* and using it for *debt*. The user for credit is not overspending, and knows it. Funds are available to pay each bill when the statement arrives. No finance charges are ever paid.

The user for debt is overspending, and knows it. When the statement arrives, the debtor will be fortunate to have the money to pay the minimum amount due — and consequently will pay the maximum interest.

One man in a California seminar told the audience that he "hadn't used his credit cards since Christmas."

"Has that been a help?" I asked.

"Golly, yes," he replied. "Otherwise I'd owe at least one thousand dollars."

2. What do you think of credit cards for most people? Since Americans owe billions of dollars to credit card companies, I think the cards are too great a temptation for most people to handle.

ON CREDIT

1. How do you establish credit without violating financial principles? The real question is: How do I develop a good credit rating and/or obtain a credit card?

Here are several steps you can take which may result in the establishment of a good credit record at your credit bureau:

a. Establish a satisfactory checking account at your local bank. Attempt to maintain a minimum balance of at least $100 at all times. Do the same for a savings account. When your banking relationship has been established, you may apply for a credit card through your bank. If you don't receive the card, the bank will tell you the reason. Then you will know future steps to take.

b. When you have saved the money for an item you wish to purchase, you're ready for another step. Let's assume you want to buy a home appliance costing between $50 and $200. Place the money you have saved in a savings account at your bank. Go to one of the national chain stores that advertise credit. Try to buy the item on an installment contract where you pay one-third or one-half as a down payment and the balance in three or four monthly installments.

When each payment is due, withdraw the money from your savings account. The interest you pay the store undoubtedly will be more than what you earn on your savings, but this difference will be your cost for establishing credit.

c. Another way is to visit a locally owned clothing, shoe, or department store where your family may be known. Request a charge account with a small limit and use it for a small credit purchase. Pay the account off in two or three payments from your savings.

d. After completing your payments, ask the credit bureau to establish a credit file on you. Do this by person or by mail. The information requested from you will include at least the following: your full name, spouse's name, present and former addresses, present and former employment, date of birth, and Social Security number. List the credit account you just paid off, along with the account number.

e. You may request from the credit bureau a copy of your file so that you know a record has been established in your name. You'll probably pay a small fee for the record, but you'll be certain you now can have your credit checked.

2. *How can we buy a house if we've never established credit?*
People have told me for years that if they don't have a good credit record, they can't buy a house. A credit bureau manager once told me no credit is the same as bad credit.

Several savings-and-loan executives dispute those statements. They've told me they are interested in the prospective buyers' bank accounts, incomes, and certainly their debt obligations. A family with no debt (and possibly no credit record) and with money saved is impressive. Such a family has made plans for the future. Their absence of debt means they can handle larger house payments than the family loaded with debt payments.

ON COSIGNING

1. What is wrong with a father cosigning a note for his son to buy a car, as a teaching device for the son? Three things are wrong:

  a. Cosigning violates Scripture: Proverbs 6:1-5, 11:15, 17:18, 20:16, 22:26, 27:13.

  b. You are teaching your son to borrow for things and violate the keep-out-of-debt principle.

  c. If you end up having to pay for the car, it's likely to cause bitterness and strained relationships (Hebrews 12:15).

2. What about cosigning with a son or daughter for college education? Our collection agency personnel have contacted hundreds of cosigners about paying the college debts of their children. The parents' reactions are almost universally resentment, bitterness, and hostility toward us for even thinking they should honor their signature and pay back the loan.

3. If cosigning violates Scripture, is lending money also against biblical principles? The Bible commands us to be lenders (Deuteronomy 15:11; Psalms 37:26, 112:5; Matthew 5:42; Luke 6:35). However, we are not to take advantage of our Christian brothers by charging interest for loans (Exodus 22:25; Leviticus 25:36; Deuteronomy 23:19).

ON INTEREST & LENDING MONEY

1. Can you shed some light and share what the Lord has taught you concerning putting money away at interest, in light of the Scriptures on usury? Is it scriptural to put money in a savings account, certificate of deposit, or other interest-bearing transaction, knowing the bank loans it out to others at interest? The Bible tells God's people to be savers. There is no question but that we aren't to spend it all, but to save some. The question is whether, biblically, we can entrust our funds to the money lenders who will pay us interest on our money. Income from loaning money usually is called *usury* in the Scriptures. Today, *usury* refers to unlawful or unjust rates.

The Bible cautions against charging interest to "the poor" and "your brother" and says we shouldn't crush our debtors with high interest rates (Psalm 15:5).

The Scriptures do not oppose lending at interest. The warnings are with reference to our willingness to lend to the needy, expecting nothing in return (see Luke 6:34). And we are not to take advantage of a poor person with the possibility of gain for ourselves (see Proverbs 28:8).

The Bible allows interest to be charged for people's wants rather than their needs. Since most credit users are making no effort to be financially free, charging them interest for their desire to have things now is not in violation of Scripture.

2. Jesus said, "Give to him who begs from you, and do not refuse him who would borrow from you" (Matthew 5:42 RSV). Is this contrary to sound financial principles? The best answer to this question I've seen is William Barclay's comment on this verse in *The Gospel of Matthew*:

> Are we then to say that Jesus urged upon men what can only be called indiscriminate giving? The answer cannot be given without qualification. It is clear that the effect of the giving on the receiver must be taken into account. Giving must never be such as to encourage him in laziness and in shiftlessness, for such giving can only hurt. But at the same time it must be remembered that many people who say that they will only give through official channels, and who refuse to help personal cases, are frequently merely producing an excuse for not giving at all, and are at all times removing the personal element from giving altogether. And it must be remembered that it is better to help a score of fraudulent beggars than to risk turning away the one man in real need.

3. Is it Christian to sell on credit? This question must be resolved, through prayer, for the Lord's leading for every laborer. Is it Christian to sell — period? Food? Many people abuse themselves by overeating the food they buy. TV sets? Need I comment? For every item sold, there is a possibility of help or harm. Personally, I can collect bills people didn't pay, but I'd not want to sell new cars on credit. Nor could I work in a finance company and lend money for high interest rates.

4. What are your views on lending money to friends? It is a quick way to lose friends and get rid of enemies. This sounds funny, but experience proves it is true. More seriously, I've found that lending individuals money when they've gotten themselves in a financial bind is an almost certain way to interfere with or postpone the work God is doing in their lives.

ON SPENDING

1. How do you advise people to handle medical expenses that go over their ability to pay? Talk over your situation with your medical creditors. Work out a plan for the steady payment of those medical bills, using some of each month's earnings.

A newspaper route man used to come to our collection agency every Monday before 8 A.M. and leave 10 dimes on the counter. Believe it or not, he paid off a hospital bill of several hundred dollars with those regular dimes.

2. How do you overcome impulsive buying? Cut up all credit cards. Close all charge accounts. When you go out shopping, carry only enough cash to buy what you have gone after. Leave your checkbook at home. Have a prayer partner with whom you share your opportunity for the Lord to strengthen you. Be accountable to your prayer partner for all money spent.

3. What if both partners in a marriage don't agree about spending money? The Bible says they can't walk together unless they agree (see Amos 3:3). There will be arguments, tension, and often open warfare. The usual result is a pile of debts they can't agree how to pay. Such pressures often will lead to divorce.

I often tell people thinking about divorce, "If you think you have money problems now, just wait until you get your divorce. Then you'll know what *real* financial problems are. The chances are that you'll both live in poverty the rest of your lives."

My straight talk seldom stops the divorce, however, because these people already have made up their minds, and the facts will not affect them.

ON THE CAR SQUEEZE

1. If you find the car you own is costing you too much money, what is the best thing to do? The writer of Proverbs had the answer for you centuries ago:

> You may have trapped yourself by your agreement. Quick! Get out of it if you possibly can! Swallow your pride; don't let embarrassment stand in the way. Go and beg to have your name erased.
> *Proverbs 6:2–3 TLB*

2. You talk about old cars being economical. A young single woman is thinking about purchasing her first car. Is it practical for her to buy an "old clunker" when she is not a mechanic? There is a lot of difference between a new car and an old clunker, both in price and in age, and most of us who drive cars are not mechanics. Some cars 10 or 20 years old cause no more trouble than certain new cars. There's also a lot of difference in price between a new car and a two- or three-year-old car—but not that much difference in utility.

3. If you can afford to buy new cars, is it wrong to drive nice cars and have nice clothes and other luxuries, especially if you are tithing? The real question concerns whether you have the nice cars, clothes, and other things, or whether these things have you. Do you love to give or do you love to get?

Faithful tithing is not automatic license for you to buy whatever you want. In our own situation, the way the Lord has blessed us, a tithe would be stingy. Our own giving goal is to have our giving exceed our living expenses. To do this, we must do without many of the "nice things we want." For Marjean and me, part of that doing without has included new cars.

4. In a business, do you recommend leasing a new car? My own company buys used cars. If you lease a car, you're paying for a new one, plus interest on the money, plus a profit for the leasing company. We buy two- to three-year-old cars with 20 to 30,000 miles on them, so we save the interest and leasing company's profit, as well as the difference between the price of the new car and the price of the used one.

5. How do you know how much to figure for transportation per mile? The best way is to gather your own figures. In chapter 5 we discussed actual operating costs for transportation. This is really an important question. My experience has proved that few people plan to spend what it really costs to run their car(s).

Some years ago I was speaking in an upper-level business class in a Christian college. For starters, I asked how many of the 12 students had cars there at the college. Ten students replied affirmatively.

Next, I asked them to tell me how much a month it was costing them to drive their cars. Silence!

As I went to the chalkboard, I began to ask them some questions. I discovered they were driving everything from an old clunker to a late-model 'Vette.

When we had finished, they had proved to me and to themselves that it was costing them an average of $150 per month to drive each of those cars. And they didn't even know it!

6. What's the best way to buy a used car? Decide how you will use the car. Decide what size and what kind of car will meet those needs. Decide how much money you want to spend. Read periodicals such as *Consumer Reports* (your local library probably has it). Study it carefully. Decide what make, model, and year of car will meet your needs. Pray for the Lord to supply the exact car to meet your needs. Then do as He leads you.

When we look for a new car for our company sales representatives, we ask God to provide a two-year-old model with the best repair record, with less than 30,000 miles on it, with one owner with whom we can talk, and for a selling price at least 35 percent below a new car of the same make. And He always has.

I remember the plan of a young couple who were involved in a college ministry. The used car they had bought several years before had more than 140,000 miles on it. The body was badly rusted; the car had no air conditioning. They had reasons to begin looking for a newer model. They were expecting their first child in a few weeks. It would certainly be more pleasant to have an air-conditioned car for the wife and baby during the approaching hot summer. Their ministry also required them to take trips of some distance with students to various conferences during the summer.

Their requirements for an automobile were well thought out. They had been searching for the past six months for a three-year-old car: a four-door with an air conditioner, having less than 30,000 miles, in excellent condition, at a price within their allotted budget.

Around the luncheon table in their home, we prayed together that God would supply a car to meet their specific requirements. Two days later I was back in Wichita talking to my neighbor. For the first time since we had prayed, I thought about my friends' need and our prayer. I asked my neighbor, "Would you happen to know anyone who has a three-year-old, air-conditioned four-door with under 30,000 miles?" I named the couple's budget price.

His reply took me by complete surprise. "I sure do," he said. He gave me the name of a man whose wife recently had won a new car. They had just decided to sell the family automobile and keep the newer car.

Excitedly, I called the man, a local realtor. As he described the car over the phone, I felt sure it was God's answer to prayer. Within a short time, I had looked at the car and found that it met all the requirements. I called the couple, and we agreed to put a deposit on the car until they could come and see it themselves. When they arrived and looked it over, we all knew God had specifically answered another prayer.

Much of the excitement of prayer involves our waiting for God's answers. Praying for financial needs usually means learning to wait expectantly for God's supply. His way often has exciting and unexpected solutions.

On the House Squeeze

The housing area has produced the most questions by my seminar participants. The most often asked question concerns whether a home mortgage violates the scriptural principle of keeping out of debt. The answer is found in chapter 6, which shows the difference between overspending and making a well-planned monthly payment that fits within your budget. Overspending results in debt. The house payment results in building an equity in your home, which becomes an asset — just the opposite of debt.

Other questions on the subject are included here.

1. What about going into debt for a house, as opposed to renting an apartment? I always give a crisp answer: "It all depends." You'll have to weigh all the factors, seek the Lord's direction, then act. Pray over such a decision and seek counsel from others.

Bear in mind that there are many advantages to apartment living. You should consider the pros and cons yourself before plunging into a long-term mortgage on a home of your own. Here are some of the advantages and disadvantages of apartment living:

Advantages of Apartment

Fixed monthly income
Freedom from responsibilities of home ownership
No unexpected repairs or maintenance
Minimum time involved in upkeep
Probable use of a swimming pool, clubhouse, sauna, etc.
No funds invested
No chance of loss on sale
No permanent commitment
Security of near neighbors during absence or presence

Disadvantages of Apartment

Builds no financial equity
No tax deductions

Less privacy
Less solitude outside
Unable to decorate as you please
Rents can be increased
Lease entanglements
No possible gain on sale
Maintenance and upkeep may be less than desired
No pride in ownership

Depending on your likes and dislikes, you may consider some advantages listed here as disadvantages, in your case (or vice-versa). The couple who don't enjoy yard work, do-it-yourself projects, and home decorating may find the apartment especially appealing. But a creative couple whose hobby is fixing things up may be very frustrated in an apartment.

Get the facts, seek godly counsel, and seek *God's* counsel.

What should you do about a house? It depends on your requirements, the real estate market, interest rates, the right house, counsel, the facts, your financial situation, and God's guidance. To find the answer, claim the Bible's telephone verse, Jeremiah 33:3: "Call unto me, and I will answer thee, and shew thee great and mighty things, which thou knowest not" (KJV).

2. *What about debts for houses?* This decision will depend on your goals. Many Christians today have the goal of becoming debt-free to the glory of God.

Long-term financial planning certainly should include a debt-free home. In our own case, we applied some of our annual savings to our mortgage payment. Since each annual additional payment applied to the principal only, each extra annual payment reduced, by more than two years, the number of years we had left to pay. It was a lot of fun to cross out those payments on that long chart and to have the mortgage paid off in half the time.

Savings money paid on your mortgage is not readily available, except at great cost and inconvenience. I'd seldom recommend that anyone put all their savings into paying off their home loan. But if you are saving regularly, and if your long-term goal is to have a mortgage-free house, then a regular, annual, additional loan payment will greatly reduce the length of your mortgage.

Beware! Some loans contain a penalty provision for pre-payment. You may be penalized for additional payments or for payments beyond a certain percentage of your loan. Check this provision before you sign any home loan or before you attempt prepayment.

3. I cosigned a note on a house for my daughter and her husband. So far there has been no problem; however, how can I get out of this? My daughter is a strong Christian, and I am the one who encouraged them to buy a house. Your counsel and your motives for your daughter and her husband seem in their best interest. However, the cosigning violated two scriptural principles: the prohibitions against cosigning in Proverbs 17:18 and the leave-and-cleave principle found in Matthew 19:5. "It is poor judgment to countersign another's note, to become responsible for his debts" (Proverbs 17:18 TLB). "... For this reason a man shall leave his father and mother and be joined to his wife, and the two shall become one . . . ." (Matthew 19:5 RSV).

Since the mortgage needed a cosigner, the lender did not feel that your daughter and her husband could handle the house. It is your financial condition that has allowed them to buy more house than they could afford.

A pastor in financial trouble came to me for counsel. When he first came to the pastorate, the church loaned him an interest-free down payment so he could buy far more house than he could afford. Several months later, his overspending had caught up with him, and he faced severe financial problems.

Possibly your daughter and her husband are in better financial condition now than when they bought the house (I surely hope they aren't in worse financial shape). The lender might now consider allowing your name to be withdrawn. It's worth a try.

ON WORKING MOTHERS

1. What about the doctors who recommend a wife work for her own therapy, even if she makes nothing in the long run? Each couple must decide the work question, before the Lord. Many women today work so the family can make ends meet. But others work primarily to make money so the family can spend more.

Work *is* good medicine. Depression usually sets in when anyone does not accept the responsibilities God has given. For the wife and mother, scriptural responsibilities include meeting the husband's needs, housekeeping, cooking, household management, and child care.

The mother who needs the exhilaration of a paycheck to meet emotional needs will possibly never be content with what that paycheck will do for her and her family. The weekly wages certainly will never do for her husband and her children what *she* could do with her creative energies applied in the home.

2. I have a part-time job and believe I do make money at it. What if a woman's creative abilities are in the area of outside work, rather than cooking, sewing and other such things? Part-time work is often a solution to a family's needs. One man came to me after buying a new house, knowing his wife needed to go to work to help meet the additional expenses of the larger house. I asked him how much additional income they needed. He didn't know. We calculated it. Would you believe their need was for less than what a half-time job would pay? Yet she had been planning to leave home for the whole day, entrust their 6-year-old to a sitter, and find the highest-paying job she could get.

We prayed for a specific part-time job between the hours of 9 A.M. and 3 P.M., within one mile of their home, that would pay enough after tithe and taxes to meet their needs.

God answered! She got the job, was home until her son left for school, and back when he returned. The neighborhood job allowed her to spend very little time driving to and from work. She liked the variety, and still had time to concentrate on the home and her family.

3. How do you feel about a mother going to work to help pay for a child's college education? I feel you should get the facts about the bottom line before you leave home to work for that purpose.

Consider your state's guidelines on family income for tuition grants. Consider the federal government's income limits for eligibility for certain government grants to students. There are many cases in which the mother's income has increased the family income to such a level that the student became ineligible for grants that would have been available based only on the father's income.

Other financial resources and tax benefits are worth looking into. Check with the school's financial aid director and with an accountant before you decide to take a job just to meet college expenses.

ON NEWLYWED FINANCIAL ISSUES

1. How can a husband suggest frugality without feeling stingy or seeming stingy to his wife? "Reliable communication permits progress" (Proverbs 13:17 TLB). A well-communicated plan for family spending should solve your problem. We all have to make choices in our spending, giving, and saving: We say *no* to this in order to say *yes* to that. If, after seeing the facts, your wife feels you are stingy, together decide which spending categories you will reduce in order to add to the category in which she feels pressure. It should not be a matter of stinginess, but of priorities.

2. What if the wife wants to tithe and the husband doesn't? What should she do? During a one-hour program in the Dallas area, where listeners were allowed to call in and ask questions, this was the most common question. The wife feels caught between the biblical principle of giving and the equally biblical principle of submission to her husband.

What should a wife do? Submit! "You wives must submit to your husbands' leadership in the same way you submit to the Lord .... So you wives must willingly obey your husbands in everything, just as the church obeys Christ" (Ephesians 5:22, 24 TLB).

By submitting, the wife leaves the husband with the responsibility for giving. This is where it belongs. When she gives herself to her husband as a helpmeet, God may use her loving-servant attitude toward his needs and her giving spirit to develop in her husband a desire to become a giver. Such a desire seldom occurs when the wife gives despite her husband's desire that she not do so.

3. I have lived by the principles you teach and have stayed out of debt. Now I have remarried, and my husband doesn't believe or follow them. How can I deal with this situation? Again, the answer is submission. God calls you to be submissive to your husband. God calls him to be responsible to Himself for the management of what money is entrusted to your family. Your prayers for your husband's obedience to God in financial principles will be a real help to your husband.

Marjean's 2¢: Husband and Wife

When our girls were little, I handled everything that had to do with them. I'd had all the child training, and George didn't know anything about it — I thought. I never gave him a chance to learn. Of course he felt awkward. He was an only child and hadn't even been around children. They looked to me for all decisions. I didn't realize I was undermining George's authority and, consequently, their respect for him. Fortunately this changed as, through some Christian teaching, I discovered my mistake.

A friend of mine had been trained in the keeping of records and handling of money. She wanted to live on a budget, but her husband showed no interest in it. So she kept records of all their expenditures. In her words, "I have three years of beautiful records, and I believe he is about ready to take charge." She hasn't pushed or nagged him about it. Instead, she has prayed and has done what she could to be ready when God got her husband's attention.

Another friend felt she could handle the record keeping much better than her husband, since he didn't like doing it. But she knew she needed to wait on the Lord's timing. Her husband was convinced scripturally that they needed to keep records, so he decided to do it. But he hated every minute of it. He would grumble, get into bad moods, and finally quit, saying, "This won't work!" But recognizing that this was God's way, that He "could do all things in Christ who strengthens him" (Philippians

> 4:13), he would go back to it.
>
> All this time, his wife was praying and trusting God. Finally, the husband came to his wife and said, "I believe this will work, and I know you like to do this kind of thing, so I would like to ask you to keep the budget book." He didn't relinquish his responsibility; instead, he delegated this particular job to one who was better equipped to handle it.

ON BUDGETING

1. How can I avoid adding to my credit card debt when it's time to buy school clothes and there's no cash available? Jesus gave us a formula: "Ask, and it will be given you...." (Matthew 7:7 RSV). So pray about the school clothes. Tell the Lord exactly what your children *need*. Purpose to trust God, not a loan. Make a list of the *essentials*. Try the thrift stores, garage sales, or other sources.

2. How do you find the balance between budgeting and making wise deals? Budgeting is planned spending which leads to wise deals. A budget will allow you to plan to buy fall school clothes at the end of winter, when they are on sale — not at the beginning of school, when they are in great demand.

3. About what percentage of your monthly income should you budget for clothing? The experts say not more than 10 percent of your spendable income should be for clothes. We find that 10 percent of our income for clothes would be exorbitant.

4. How do you know how much to allow for income tax, when each year your earnings increase and you owe more than your estimated taxes? Figure what percent of your total income last year's state and federal taxes were. Whenever your current month's income exceeds last year's income, set aside in a special savings account that same percent of the additional income. Then you'll probably be prepared at tax time.

5. *How can a budget be worked out for a person whose income is irregular in amount and never catches up with present obligations? Where is the handle?* Every successful budget has a handle: The income is greater than the expenditures. If income *never* catches up with present obligations, the spending must be cut.

6. *Our income is flexible, as my husband is self-employed (he's a doctor). It seems impossible to have a budget and keep it on target. Any suggestions?* Plan your spending on a level monthly budget. Withdraw from his practice, each month, the amount you plan to spend. Put the rest in savings. If he earns less in a month than you plan to spend, withdraw the difference from your savings.

7. *How long should you keep records?* With a single budget book for each year of our marriage, I see no reason to destroy them. You may want to write a book someday about your experiences.

8. *How much should a family of five (three small children) allow for groceries?* Typically, food costs from 20 percent down to 12 percent of gross income, with the higher percentages starting with the lower incomes and decreasing to the higher incomes.

9. *Do you practice what you tell us, to the last detail? What is the reaction of your family to your budget? Do you stand fast and carry this out now?* Questions often are asked about whether we live what we write and speak about. We try to. Marjean and I have enjoyed the profit from a lifetime of budgeting. It has enabled us to reach our goal of giving the Lord more than we spend for living expenses. That's why we still stand fast to a budget now.

Marjean's Response

I want to comment about the question of whether we practice what we teach.

A few years ago, George suggested that perhaps, since we had been keeping a budget for several years and our finances

> seemed in good shape, we could do away with the labor of keeping a budget.
>
> I protested immediately. Having worked at this plan for so many years, I was beginning to learn how to let it work for me.
>
> In the clothes category, I know exactly how much money I have to spend or need to save in order to buy an article of clothing. In the food category, I plan the amount of the check I write each week, in order to stay within the allotted amount.
>
> I just don't know how I could operate without a budget! I certainly wouldn't want to try.

10. How do you set up a budget for a person who has never had any practice in keeping records? Start simply. Try to plan one spending category, such as food. Keep track of all cash spent and checks written for all food purchases. Then compare food spending to the plan. Once it has been done in one area, it can be done in all others.

11. How do you make a decision on spending money for maintenance of someone else's well-meaning offer of a gift to you? Before receiving a gift, count the cost. I once turned down the gift of a country club membership because, among other reasons, I did not want to spend money on the monthly dues.

12. What is depreciation? Is it any use to family budget planning? How? Depreciation is the difference between what you pay for an item and what it can be sold for at any given time. The best use in the family budget is to plan to set aside enough money to be able to replace items that will wear out, such as the car, washer, dryer, air conditioner, furnace, and a host of other items.

13. How do you keep financially on top of bills if your husband's job is seasonal or unstable at times? His job pays well when he works, but usually we can almost count on at least a month-and-a-half off each year. Total your annual income. Divide that figure by the 10 months he works, to see how to plan your monthly spending. During the months he works, set aside in a savings account all his income over a monthly spending plan. During the "off" months, you should have enough to withdraw for your spending needs.

14. *How can I keep a balanced budget?* A "balanced budget" means income at least equals spending. Most people balance their budgets by controlling their spending.

15. *Is it necessary to write down everything I spend in order to be on a budget?* Not necessarily. Example: Write a check for $50 for food. Keep the money in a separate coin purse, and always use it only for food. You write down only the $50 check in your budget book. When your coin purse is empty, you know that the $50 has gone for food. There's no need to keep track of where you spent it. But be honest.

16. *How can I know where my money is going if the budget doesn't balance?* Only by keeping records of your spending can you know where your money is going. This is true regardless of whether you balance your budget.

17. *Do you have any information regarding the establishment of a realistic budget that could be used in a family? Oftentimes people either overestimate or underestimate their financial capabilities and use of their income.* A budget is a series of financial goals for a particular family. Each family will set their own goals, based on their own priorities. For example, our family always placed our home higher in the spending category than our car. Consequently, our home has been more than adequate, while our cars all have been bought used.

We valued savings for education more highly than clothes or furniture. Consequently, we had funds set aside for college for our daughters, but we did without many clothing wants and bought lots of used furniture, carpets, and other household items.

Each family must make their own choices, and you must face the facts of your own situation.

18. Why are records of past payments important in knowing where your money went? Without records, you'll deceive yourself on where your money really goes. When I give people the assignment to record all their spending for a week, they are always amazed at how much money they're spending on meaningless items.

With records, you'll spot errors more easily. One month, at my business, one of my incoming toll-free telephone bills more than doubled. By producing records for my previous six months of bills, I showed the phone company that my current bill was unreasonable. Sure enough, their computer had gone awry.

Records settle disputes, save time, and help in future planning.

19. How can you best plan a budget without really knowing what the cost of living and other expenditures will be? With living costs rising regularly, budgeting is a necessity. Each year's spending plan includes increases in certain spending areas. For example, within the same living quarters, you would need to plan on spending a larger amount than you spent last year for utilities.

20. How do you handle budgets for teen-agers? The goal of a child's budget is to help him or her learn to be a responsible money manager. Our daughters started out with the three-box cash system: Every allowance was divided into three boxes — church, save, spend.

By the time children are in high school, they should be ready for a more involved but realistic budget. A full teen-age spending plan could include church, savings, clothes, gifts, health, education, fun, and transportation.

A budget in college could be similar to that of the high schooler, with some items added. They'll need stamps, stationery, laundry money, and myriad other items, if they live away from home.

21. What did your daughters do with money they earned while they were on a budget? Our daughters divided the earnings according to a predetermined plan. A good division is among giving, saving, and spending. An excellent plan is to give 10 percent, save 40 percent and spend 50 percent. What they spend *their* money on with that kind of plan should be up to *them*.

22. *What about college students whose basic expenses come to more than they can earn in a part-time job?* Students, too, face situations in which expenses exceed income. Several alternatives exist:

- If you are trusting God for the money to get you through school and there just isn't enough money, you could conclude that, at this time, the Lord wants you some place other than school.
- You could quit trusting God and trust a loan to "tide you over."
- You could pray for God to multiply your willingness to work. With studying and part-time work occupying the bulk of your time, you see no way to add to your work. Here's where "my God will supply every need of yours" (Philippians 4:19 RSV) comes in.

Tell the Lord you're willing to be in school or out, as He leads (see Psalm 32:8). Ask the Lord for income sufficient to pay for your schooling (see Matthew 7:7). Be alert to opportunities for you to earn while you learn. Many jobs today require your presence more than your work. House-sitting while people are away earns you income while you have time to study. Funeral homes usually require someone on duty at night to answer the telephone.

Make use of your school breaks. Thanksgiving, Christmas, and spring break offer times for extra earnings.

23. *What do you think about school loans?* My collection agency has tried to collect more than 20,000 delinquent school loans that have been turned over to us by almost 100 colleges. Most of these loans were granted in the haste of college registration. Seldom is much counseling done about the responsibility of repayment. My experience is that most students don't really understand what they are facing when they sign a note to pay back a large debt, plus interest, over a 10-year period after they graduate.

On a delinquent account in our office, our first telephone contact produced a violent reaction from a girl who owed money to a Christian college. She raved about how she already had paid $200 and her semester at school certainly hadn't been worth that amount. She was hostile to us and critical of the college. She even said school officials had lied to her about the cost of the school. Her tirade ended by her claiming that she would not pay the $1,200 the school said she owed and that the school wouldn't sue her, since it would not be a Christian act for the school to file suit against her, a Christian.

A review of her file at school showed a radical change in her attitude since she had married. Before that time, she had made regular, small payments on the loan. With each payment she had written to thank the school for her education. She also had acknowledged her financial obligation to the school and promised faithful payments for as long as it took to pay off what she owed.

Then came the dramatic change. This is just one example of what the trauma and pressure can do to young couples with school debts. As they turn their thoughts toward things for their home, they easily forget their promises of the past.

How easy it is, in the process, to turn away from the Lord, as well. "For the love of money is the first step toward all kinds of sin. Some people have even turned away from God because of their love for it, and as a result have pierced themselves with many sorrows" (1 Timothy 6:10 TLB).

24. What do you do when people make unusual requests for your money—for example, college students who have run out of money and want to borrow some? God may choose you to meet a brother or sister's need. If, after prayer, you have peace about *giving* the person the money, then give it joyfully.

My own experience is that God often uses finances to teach people spiritual lessons. Unfaithfulness with finances often results in a person's being in a position of real need. By looking to the *Lord* to meet that need, they learn valuable lessons of prayer and faith. By looking to other *people* to meet the need, they miss such lessons and spiritual growth.

I've had to ask the Lord's forgiveness more than once for giving someone money and preventing the work God was doing in his life. When a repossessor came to my office to pick up an employee's car, I interfered. Money the Lord had entrusted to me was used to prevent the repossession. I felt I was helping my employee. Later, I discovered she could not afford her car, but was unwilling to give it up. In spite of me and her, God allowed the car to be totaled some days later — an even tougher way to give it up!

25. What if parents really want a student to take out a loan for college, and the student does not want to and shows them why (biblical reasons), and prays, but they still feel the loan is necessary? Take out the loan. God will bless your obedience to your parents. The Bible commands you to obey your parents, and ends with the promise "that it may be well with you" (Ephesians 6:1–3 NEB).

26. If you commit yourself to supporting certain ministries and your income is reduced, what should you do? Lower your support. We are to be proportionate givers: income up, giving up; income down, giving down.

27. What should we give if we have no income? Tithe your time.

ON BEING CONTENT

1. If you are content with what you have, how do you get ahead? Why work if you are content? We are told in the Bible to be content with what we *have*, not what we are (see Hebrews 13:5). Our task is to work heartily, as serving the Lord and not men. With a servant attitude toward our employers, we can expect to receive promotions to greater responsibilities.

2. Can a young person who feels a call to the Christian ministry be content with less than an optimum education, because of financial limitations? Paul instructs us by example to be content "in every situation, whether it be a full stomach or hunger, plenty or want" (Philippians 4:12 TLB). Can you imagine Paul's feeling limited because he didn't have a graduate degree from the top Christian seminary?

3. Does being content with what you have mean we are wrong in trying to improve our present financial standing? The biblical principle is that we reap what we sow. Work often is equated with prosperity in the Bible (see Proverbs 14:23, 28:19). If the Lord wants to entrust you with more money, He'll do it most often through your efforts at work.

4. How do you balance being content with having a drive to do better in life and being a success at business? What is your goal? Jesus said if you "seek first his kingdom and his righteousness... all these things shall be yours as well" (Matthew 6:33 RSV). Obey God and obey your employer. Serve God and serve your customers. That's the formula for success.

ON BUSINESS LOANS

1. Would you explain the difference (if there is any) between personal financing and business financing and the use of debt (or borrowed) capital in each? Personal financing most often means borrowing for consumption. A family *wants* a new car, washer, furniture, or other household item. Without the cash, the item is bought, and the amount it cost is charged. Or, some budget buster crops up: repairs for the car, the furnace, water heater, or washer. With no money saved, the repair is made with borrowed money. Such borrowing is for consumption. The biblical principle of making do with your pay is being violated (see Luke 3:14).

Business borrowing is often for production tools. A new machine is purchased with borrowed funds. The machine will produce items which may be sold at a profit, which will be used to repay the loans. And the production machine will be security for the loan.

The difference is between borrowing for consumption and borrowing for production. An illustration of business borrowing is the purchase of my computer. The use of the computer was projected to reduce our employee needs by two. These savings in labor did materialize. The wages saved could have been used to pay for the computer, had we borrowed the money to purchase it.

2. How do you start a business if you don't presently have the money? The biggest single reason people don't start businesses is that they don't have the money. Two ways to obtain the money are to borrow it or to get someone to invest in the business. Since most businesses don't make a profit until the business has been established for several months, or even years, much money is needed to pay the expenses during those first profitless months. The passages of Scripture in which debt is mentioned all appear to refer to personal debt.

3. What do you think about a farmer borrowing tens of thousands of dollars for farm machinery? One problem with borrowing is that the purchase frequently is for more than would have been bought if a certain amount of cash had been saved for the purpose. The farmer who saves $25,000 for a tractor probably will look until he finds one he thinks will do the job for the $25,000 he has. The farmer who buys what he wants on credit may end up with an air-conditioned cab, complete with AM-FM stereo, which may not be that necessary.

On Church Finances

1. How can a local church teach its members financial responsibility? A body of believers meeting in a certain location becomes a local church. Financial principles for individuals are applicable to groups of God's people. The local congregation which recognizes its opportunity to give away the first part of all the church income is following the biblical principle of giving the first fruits to the Lord. That congregation also sets an example of the giving-first principle for individual members. The congregation which pays all the bills first and then gives what is left (if any) to missions and the work of the Lord outside the local church is setting a poor example for its members.

2. Should a church go into debt to build a new building? When I asked one of my friends, who is the stewardship leader of his denomination, what he thought about church debt, he answered, "There are two things I dislike about church debt: There's the principle — and the interest."

An individual with a need faces the question, "Trust God or trust a loan?" So does a congregation.

I've seen the ministry of many churches stifled for years while members conducted fund drive after fund drive to raise more money to pay on the mortgage of the "new building." I certainly don't subscribe to the theory I've heard advanced: "A congregation that always has a debt will be the most active."

There have been many thrilling stories of God's power and provision told by congregations who trusted God for a debt-free building. And what an example such a project is to the individual members.

Christian Financial Concepts published an excellent pamphlet titled "Should Churches Borrow Money?" Here is a portion of that material, written by Larry Burkett.

> IS CHURCH BORROWING SCRIPTURAL? This question must first be approached from the "absolutes." God's Word does not say that borrowing on the part of the "church" is forbidden.
>
> However, borrowing represents the LEAST rather than the BEST as the church is commanded to observe. In many fellowships the existence of an indebtedness pressures them into an attitude of debt first — God second. In Proverbs 22:7, it is stated that the borrower is servant to the lender. The very act of borrowing places the church in bondage to an authority other than God's.
>
> Nowhere in God's Word did He ever manifest Himself through a loan. He promises to supply ALL of our needs (Philippians 4:19). Therefore the very act of borrowing is the outer sign of an inner doubt.
>
> GOD'S BUILDING PLAN. The first time God directed a building to be constructed was in the wilderness, "Tell the sons of Israel to raise a contribution for me; from every man whose heart moves him you shall raise my contribution" (Exodus 25:2).
>
> Thus God directed the people to give. In Exodus 36:6, Moses actually had to direct the people to stop giving. One of the unifying factors bringing the Jews into closer fellowship both with God and each other was the common goal God set

before them.

In 1 Chronicles 29, David describes the collection for God's temple. It is clear that loans were not necessary to build God's house. Verse 14 describes this plan: God's people, sharing in God's plan, with God's money.

WHY NOT BORROW? The church is called by God to be unique, set apart from the world. Therefore, whatever the norm is in the world, the church must follow a totally different path.

In Philippians 2:15, we are told to hold ourselves above reproach, that we may be lights into the world of darkness. The way the church handles its money is one of the best (or poorest) testimonies. Unfortunately, many churches today operate on a nearly parallel path to secular institutions.

In a financial sense, what testimony does a church that borrows have over a secular company? Remember, the church is to be set apart, unique and established solely to God's glory.

IS BORROWING TRUSTING GOD? Does it require more faith to believe God for monthly payments or to believe He can supply according to the need "beforehand?" Borrowing is a subtle way to buffer God's will for our lives. It does not necessarily represent an overt sin but it does reflect that a church is willing to accept the LEAST financially rather than the BEST. In reality the people are being denied God's blessings, both spiritually and financially. Assuming that it is God's will for a church to build, He will supply the resource to do so. When God supplies, He often provides an abundance beyond what is actually needed (2 Corinthians 9:8).

A REASONABLE COMPROMISE. Obviously, not every church is at the same level of spiritual and financial maturity. A generation of borrowing habits are not easy to overcome and thus discerning believers must seek a reasonable compromise to avoid internal conflict.

It is clear that borrowing from unbelievers is not only a poor witness but unscriptural. In 3 John 1:7–8 believers are admonished to support those who bring the Word for "they accept nothing from the unsaved."

How can a church be a witness to God's glory and promise while they have to ask the unsaved to lend the money even for their meeting place?

A reasonable compromise is to borrow from God's people

through bonds or some other means. At least then God's people supply and receive His money. (The fact that this is a common means of fund building programs testifies that the resources are available.)

OUTER REFLECTION. Remember that the way a church raises and administers its money is but an outer reflection of the inner conviction.

CHALLENGE. It is a fact that most of the building programs that are truly needed could be funded by the Christians involved surrendering less than TEN PERCENT of their savings. They don't either because of a lack of commitment or borrowing is made too easy an alternative.

Our faith does not grow stronger unless it is tried and tested (James 1:3–4). The same is true with our financial faith.

3. Does the church have any responsibility to the welfare problem?

Some years ago I heard that if every church would care for a small number of welfare recipients, no one would need to be on welfare. I decided to develop some figures for the county where I live. Dividing the number of churches into the number of welfare cases, I discovered each church would need to have responsibility for 18 cases.

Think how exciting it would be if every congregation had members who considered it their responsibility to care for those few needy families in their own community. Caring would mean more than doling out the money needed to subsist. First would come individual attention, learning of needs, building a trusting relationship. Then the opportunity to share Jesus would come.

Practical needs could be met with surplus from other church members. The people on welfare could be taught to work, to plan menus, to keep a budget. We'd be taking a "cup of cold water" to the thirsty. They could be integrated into the fellowship of Jesus Christ.

4. How do you feel about churches and Christian organizations that ask you to give in order to pay debts accumulated when income fell?

What a contrast! How different can appeals be? I remember one Christian television personality's emotional appeals for money to pay debts accumulated in building projects. The audience was threatened by the thought that unless money was sent *now*, the building project would be lost and the ministry would stop. Contrast that to a quotation from Dr. Victor B. Nelson of the Billy Graham Evangelistic Association: "The Billy Graham Evangelistic Association does not go into debt. We have always paid our bills on time and have expanded and proceeded only as the Lord has blessed and guided."

God's plan for His family is financial freedom. If God's people aim to be financially free, then how much more necessary is it for God's gathered family (the local church) to stay financially free.

ON GIVING

1. What do you mean by percentage giving? Proportionate giving means deciding on a percentage of your income to give to the Lord's work. If you adopt the tithe, you give 10 percent of your income. "Upon the first day of the week let every one among you lay by him in store, as God hath prospered him, that there be no gatherings when I come" (1 Corinthians 16:2 KJV). Percentage giving is a way of determining the amount you give by setting aside a percentage of your income. The size of your income is how God has prospered you.

For a number of years Marjean and I have given 15 percent of our income to a certain level. As God has prospered us, we have given 25 percent of the amount beyond that level.

We've known others who have a graduated upward scale, increasing their giving percentage with each increment in earnings.

2. Do you always have to give to the church? My answer to that question is usually another question: How do you define "the church?" My own definition of the church is much broader than the building on the corner, where we worship.

3. What is the Christian's perspective of meeting needs of the poor —the scriptural basis as individuals and as society? Solomon said, "To help the poor is to honor God" (Proverbs 14:31 TLB). The Bible even says happiness belongs to the generous man who feeds the poor (see Proverbs 22:9). God promises to meet our needs, if we give to the poor.

The Scriptures make it clear that Christians are directed to do more than talk about the poor (see James 2:15, 16). Your own local church may be involved with feeding and clothing some nearby and distant poor persons. If not, you may be led by God to give directly to the poor God puts on your doorstep or to an organization that has a ministry to the poor.

4. Would it be right to borrow money to give, say, to a church building program? Borrowing money to give presumes on God. Scripturally, our giving is based on how God has prospered us, not the need of the appeal. God does not ask us to give out of what we don't have; we are to give only out of what He has entrusted to us. "You will always be rich enough to be generous" (2 Corinthians 9:11 NEB). Note that Paul did not say, "Your credit always will be enough so you can give generously."

5. What do you think about faith pledges? A faith pledge is a commitment to give money that is not in sight to a certain person or organization. There are two sides to a faith pledge:

- Your pledge to give.
- Your faith that God will provide.

If God does not provide income beyond your expected earnings, then your pledge need not be kept.

My own faith pledge experience has been exciting. I once received from a close Christian brother an invitation to invest funds in an innovative new way to reach businessmen for Christ. At the time, we'd committed all the funds for the year that we could reasonably expect and had made a substantial faith pledge besides. I can remember writing to the brother and sharing that not only was I committed, but that I didn't have the faith that God would provide the pledge, let alone enough to give to his project. Oh, ye of little faith! Before the year was over, in spite of my lack of faith, God did provide the entire faith pledge, with enough left over to send a generous check to the brother, as well as some additional gifts.

ON SCRIPTURAL CONTRADICTIONS

1. If we are to trust God to supply our every need, does it show a lack of trust to put money into such things as life and health insurance, instead of putting that money into Christian charities and programs? The Bible does say God will supply our needs. There's no reason that supply can't come through various kinds of insurance, however.

Solomon said, "A prudent man foresees the difficulties ahead and prepares for them; the simpleton goes blindly on and suffers the consequences" (Proverbs 22:3 TLB).

God's Word never tells us we won't be sick or suffer from disease. Medical insurance provides a plan for the prudent person to pay for illness. By making a monthly premium payment, a person is budgeting for future medical expenses. I carry medical insurance and also provide part of the premium for my coworkers to obtain good major medical coverage at the lowest group rates.

Life insurance is a way to make provision for your family in case of the death of the wage earner. The person who cares enough for his or her family to purchase life insurance is expressing a unique brand of love.

One woman who came to me for financial counseling told me this story. At the time her daughter was preparing to leave for college, her husband died. His life insurance made it possible for the woman to buy a house in the college town, where she and her daughter could live together. Since the woman had eye trouble and couldn't work, the life insurance made the difference between a poverty existence and continuing a lifestyle similar to their past one. I've never seen anyone who was collecting life insurance proceeds who could be anything but thankful for the unselfishness of the deceased loved one.

Disability insurance can be equally important. A far better name for it is income protection insurance. When the wage earner becomes unable to work because of sickness or accident, after a waiting period of several days to several months, the insurance begins to provide income payments.

My own company carries such insurance for our company family. Scripturally, I have a responsibility to them to meet their needs in times of crisis. What a blessing to know the incomes of several disabled employees have continued long after they were unable to work.

2. *Do you think a person with family responsibilities should quit a job because he believes God is calling him to study for the ministry?* The first question I would ask is, "What kind of ministry does the person with family responsibilities have where he is?"

- Is his marriage alive and well?
- Is he the priest in his own family?
- Are his children being taught by conduct and example in prayer and the study of God's Word?
- Is he functioning as a multiplying, fruitful Christian where he is working now?
- Are people being led to Christ?
- Are Christians being encouraged and shown how to grow?
- Are the fruits of the Spirit so evident in the person's life that coworkers are coming to him for counsel?

I've heard Dr. Richard Halverson say many times, "If you aren't functioning for Jesus Christ where you are, you probably won't function for Christ where you're not."

If your work life is fruitful now and you sense God's leading to study for the ministry, seek godly counsel. Also seek the counsel of your own family. And be certain your wife's honest feelings are being communicated to you.

ON GIVING AFTER YOU LIVE

1. *Is a lawyer necessary to draw up a will?* Do you need a surgeon to perform surgery? I can't imagine a do-it-myself will or my will being copied from a friend's will (which may have been drawn up by a lawyer). Would I take my friend's prescribed pills?

2. *In writing a will, do you think the lawyer should be a Christian?* The preference is to deal with a Christian, because the psalmist indicates we'll be blessed if we walk not in the counsel of the ungodly (see Psalm 1:1). But if there are no Christians around, pick a competent attorney. Not all attorneys are competent estate planners. Inquire of your accountant, insurance officer, or bank trust officer for the name of an attorney who has handled a high volume of estate planning work.

3. What should be included in a will? Ask your attorney and/or read estate planning literature prepared by a Christian lawyer. It is *your* will; let it reflect *you*. Since wills are read by several people, and often are read for generations, in abstracts, some Christians even include their personal testimonies.

one hundred **199** *ninety-nine*

WAYS TO SAVE MONEY

1. Subscribe to *The Penny Pincher* newsletter:
P.O. Box 809
Kings Park, NY 11754
516-724-1868
Annual subscription rate: $12.00

2. Cut up one or more credit cards.

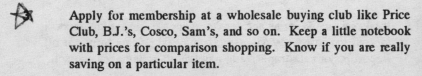 Apply for membership at a wholesale buying club like Price Club, B.J.'s, Cosco, Sam's, and so on. Keep a little notebook with prices for comparison shopping. Know if you are really saving on a particular item.

Stay high and dry with cloth diapers. Compared to disposables, cloth diapers may save almost $1,000 and fourteen trees per child!

5. Got the end of the month, where'd my money go blues? Here are two plans of action. You can earn $6,000 more per year, but after taxes you'll take home considerably less, or you can cut back on spending and save $6,000 . . . without paying one cent to Uncle Sam.

6. Brighten your holiday budget by recycling old Christmas cards. Make postcards, leaving a space on the right-hand side for the address and 19-cent stamp, and include your own greeting.

7. Once considered almost luxury items, furniture and computers may be within your reach if you buy used. Check the local shopping news, or network with friends who know the places and people to call.

8. Waste the wheels! If you have an extra car that you don't really

need, sell it and invest the money wisely or pay off debts. Then sit back and watch your insurance costs drop while you enjoy additional savings on gasoline and repairs.

9.   Don't reach deep into the deep freeze: A full freezer means greater efficiency and savings. To take up space, store such items as flour, rice, pasta, and beans in the freezer (the foods will not be harmed).

10.   Make your home more energy efficient by draining your gas (not electric) water heater periodically. Experts recommend draining one pail every three months to remove sediment from bottom of tank.

11.   It takes a second for an accident to happen . . . but if you report it to your car insurance company, it may take years to pay it off. Report major catastrophes and pay the other damages yourself.

12.   Become a quick-change artist. When you come home from work change your clothes before beginning household chores. Avoid wrinkles by hanging clothes properly and you'll save weekly on dry cleaning.

13.   Steer clear of expensive window cleaners. In an empty spray bottle add a small amount of dishwashing liquid and fill with ammonia.

14.   Extend (indefinitely!) the life of your best-quality shoes. Don't wear the same pair day after day, use unfinished cedar shoe trees, apply shoe cream once a week, and use sole protectors.

15.   Every die-hard garage sale scavenger needs sustenance. Be sure to sell sodas, popcorn, and other snacks at your next bargain bonanza.

16.   Save on garbage bags by recycling, recycling, recycling! Avoid purchasing processed foods with extra packaging and be sure to crush cereal, cracker, and cookie cardboard boxes.

17. "I'll take a raincheck." Say those four words the next time your supermarket runs out of an advertised sale item, and reap the benefits when prices go up again.

18. The "perennial favorites" also mean perennial savings. Instead of planting annual flowers, plant perennials and see them come up each year and multiply. Every three years you will have doubled the number of plants and blooms. Split them and move to other flower beds or share with friends, or even sell some for pin money!

19. Think before you drive! Save on gasoline by writing down errands in a logical order so you don't backtrack or drive out of your way.

20. "Second Hand Rose" is no stigma anymore. Buy your children's clothing at a consignment shop and enjoy major savings on famous label items that perhaps were only worn one season.

21. No peeking! Every time you open the oven door, the temperature inside drops 25 degrees.

22. You don't have to wear black to be known as "Johnny Cash." If you habitually pay cash for as many purchases as possible, you'll see immediately how much money you are spending and how much you have left, two qualities of a conservative and shrewd financial planner.

23. After you've listened to a salesperson's spiel about the benefits of appliance service contracts, do what many experts advise. Say no thanks.

24. Develop the killer instinct when it comes to debt! Because savings accounts have low interest rates compared with credit card or loan rates, use savings to begin paying off debts.

25. Do you feel compelled to purchase extra insurance when you're waiting for the keys to a rental car? Each time you rent a car you

get free collision-damage insurance if you charge the car to a gold MasterCard/Visa or American Express card, or if your permanent car insurance policy contains that coverage. To be absolutely sure of your coverage, check with your insurance agent.

26. *En famille*, the French say. Involve the entire family when tackling unnecessary debt by taking less expensive and extensive vacations, chipping in when needed, and giving gifts of service, not material items.

27. Make homemade bread for 50 cents a loaf! If you are buying flour and yeast in bulk, pay only 15 cents per loaf. Buy one-pound packages of instant yeast from a health food store and save big over those packets from the supermarket. Be sure and store yeast in the refrigerator.

28. Learn how to work a supermarket! Stock up on each week's meats on sale and ask butchers if they give discounts on the ends of deli meats or if they mark down older cuts.

29. Here's another tip for the supermarket terminator (*you*). Say "hasta la vista" to high produce prices by picking up damaged produce that the store routinely boxes and discards.

30. Credit card caveat: Never put your credit card number on a personal check, even when making a credit payment. Someone could apply for credit in your name.

31. You don't have to be a rocket scientist to decipher your monthly telephone bills, just a penny-pinching watchdog. Cancel such "add-on" charges as call waiting, call forwarding, touchtone service, and so on if you do not use them enough to warrant the costs.

32. Remember the toaster oven you got as a wedding gift or as a desperation gift from some twice-removed relative? Ideal for small snacks or lunch, this convenient appliance does not have to be preheated, will save on electricity, and heats the house less

than a conventional oven.

33. Home improvements are just that, for the home. Apartment improvements are for the landlord.

34. Billions of dollars of student financial assistance from private sources go unused each year. If you're intent on scaling those ivied walls, ask a reference librarian or contact a local college consultant service for application information.

35. Too much, too late? You may be turned down for a car loan and mortgage if you have many credit cards, most with a sizeable outstanding balance.

36. When is debt OK? If you're borrowing for a business, an education, a house, a car for work, in short, for *an investment*, that's OK. But don't borrow for things you'll consume.

37. You can have "House Beautiful" even if you're in the poorhouse. Purchase fabric and wallpaper from discount chains or through 800 numbers found in the back pages of magazines, and then *do it yourself*!

38. Use your senior status to qualify for prescription drug discounts. Some states (e.g., NY and PA) even have drug discount programs.

39. "No thank you." Three words that may be said when your credit card company chooses without your consent to increase your credit limit.

40. What's in a name? Don't forget generic and store-brand over-the-counter drugs when purchasing aspirin, antidiarrheals, and antihistamines, to name a few.

41. Try the breakfast of penny pinchers! Instead of pricey cold breakfast cereals, substitute cooked oatmeal (not instant), cooked rice, waffles and pancakes (both homemade), muffins, or eggs and toast. If you must have cold cereal, generic cereals taste as good at half

the price.

42.   Are you user thrifty? If you're considering upgrading your computer word processing program, save 50 percent or more by taking advantage of upgrade offers in computer magazines and some software stores.

43.   Recycled petals? Flower arrangements can sometimes be had for free by calling local funeral homes and asking for their discards.

44.   Protect your money automatically. Never leave automated teller machine (ATM) receipts around the machine after a transaction. Your account number can be used by criminals to withdraw *your* funds.

45.   Plug into the outlet craze! Designer fashions, bone china, and other home accoutrements can be had for much less at manufacturers' outlets.

46.   It's never too early to teach fiscal responsibility. Instead of buying toys on demand for your kids or grandkids, encourage youngsters to ask for those items for their birthdays and Christmas.

47.   No sleeping in! High school and college-age children should be encouraged to seek summer employment. The work ethic will always hold them in good stead.

48.   A dollar or two doesn't buy much anymore but it can still burn a hole in your child's pocket. If children choose to spend their weekly allowance, encourage them to comparison shop (welcome to our world!).

49.   Personal finance math 101: To determine how many years it will take for an investment to double in value, divide the rate of return (percent) into 72.

50.   Go with the flow when food shopping. First make a list of items

you need and then pick up the store flyer and buy dinner items based only on what's on sale. Stock up when it's within your grocery budget.

51. Remember the humble clothespin? Yes, it's another money saver from your past. Save 50 cents to one dollar a load when you dry clothes on a line or drying rack instead of in the electric dryer. Two loads a week dried without the dryer saves $50 to $104 per year, four loads saves $100 to $208 a year, and so on.

52. One day you just may leave home without it. Keep in a safe place a list of your credit card numbers, expiration dates, and the telephone numbers of each card issuer in case you lose a card or it is stolen.

53. What should you tell your boss when you think you've earned a raise? Throughout the year write down your accomplishments as they occur and present them at the time of your review.

54. Are you in hot water? Since 90 percent of a washing machine's energy goes toward heating water, use hot water sparingly and spend less using warm and cold. (You'll also save by only running full loads.)

55. How low can you go? Comparison shop at different local supermarkets each week for a month. At each store write down prices of items you buy regularly and keep these prices handy for future reference. Then choose as your weekly supermarket the store where you saved the most.

56. Checked out your new health club yet? It's just outside your door, the great outdoors, that is, and you'll save a bundle by working out there.

57. Keep it in the family. If at all possible, ask a family member to serve as executor of your estate.

58. Rein in that horsepower—by driving cars designed for the street,

not the speedway, within the speed limit—and save hundreds of dollars each year. We're talking traffic ticket fees, gasoline costs, and higher insurance premiums.

59. Most museums and zoos have yearly family rates. Such outings are educational, enjoyable, and far less costly than movies or amusement parks.

60. More supermarket savvy: In general you'll save more by focusing on the front and back pages of the store flyer than on the inside pages.

61. Preventative medicine includes healthy eating habits. Save big on medical bills for your family by avoiding processed foods and eating fresh fruit and vegetables and whole grain products.

62. Your local library may be the best-kept savings secret in town. Besides the usual (books!), patrons can check out videos (often for free or nominal cost), magazines, CDs, and cameras. While there take advantage of personal computers and typewriters.

63. If to err is human, then to doublecheck restaurant and hotel bills is a must.

64. Where have I seen that before? Clothes that are dated, worn, or outgrown can be cut up and used to make quilts and comforters.

65. Anticipation is one key to savings. Instead of purchasing items of need last minute at a high-priced convenience store, think ahead and buy at a discount mart.

66. Reduce the term on your mortgage by paying a little extra each month. For example, on a $75,000 thirty-year mortgage at 10 percent interest, an extra $25 per month will save you more than $34,000 in interest. Call your mortgage company for details.

67. Homemade baby food involves no secret formulas. Simply process your own cooked vegetables in the blender or food

processor and spoon puréed mixture into an ice tray. Freeze, then pop veggie cubes into a pan and heat and serve.

 Invest in a water-efficient showerhead and save. Reports show savings of $20 to $30 per year for a family of three with just that small adjustment.

 The time by any other name would be as accurate? (Apologies to Shakespeare!) Inexpensive watches look as good and work as well as extremely expensive ones. Buy two or three bargain watches in different styles and still save hundreds of dollars you might have spent on a trendier timepiece.

70. Anticipation revisited: Read *Consumer Reports* and like publications before purchasing items of need. You'll find a quality product with a desirable price tag.

71. Does the thought of an expensive swingset send you sliding into bankruptcy? The budget choice: Hang a rope swing from a sturdy tree branch. (A board can be used for the seat or you can use a tire.) Be sure the swing is hung in a safe location and then sit back and watch your future Olympians have a great time.

72. The lights are on . . . and somebody's home! By using fluorescent lightbulbs instead of incandescent ones you'll reduce electrical bills and protect the environment.

73. Be strong and of great courage! Never be afraid to bargain . . . at any store, for any product.

74. To your health! An eight-ounce glass of water can be refilled thousands of times for the same cost as several cans of soda.

75. "Put it in writing." (What to say to telemarket callers)

76. Other grocery aisle advice: When the quality of items doesn't vary much, e.g., flour, sugar, and other staples, always buy the cheapest products. Be sure to weigh fresh produce as those pounds

tend to add up quickly.

77. Save money, the ozone layer, and more! Walk to do most errands and, if you can't walk there, carpool or take a bus to work.

78. Income tax time rolls around too quickly each year. Bankers advise not to pay your taxes too far in advance and let those dollars work for you, not Uncle Sam.

79. Standby travelers know from experience. The most economical way to take an ocean cruise is to put your name on the list.

80. Become auto-smart. Purchase your next used car for an amount between loan value and wholesale (get a copy of NADA from a banker), but only after a reliable mechanic gives his or her OK.

81. Bulk up and slim down that food budget. Buy foods in bulk and then split with friends if you can't use so much or don't have room to store such large quantities (don't forget your freezer!).

82. Stop smoking cigarettes . . . and sock away each week the money you would have spent on them. A pack-a-day habit could add up to $700 per year!

83. Imagine your yard as you've always wanted it . . . without paying for a landscape service?? The National Arbor Day Foundation will send you an assortment of trees or bushes free upon receipt of $10 membership fee (write: 100 Arbor Ave., Nebraska City, NE 68410).

84. Paper towels absorb more than liquid. Save by using sponges.

85. Clothes shopping is almost a national pastime, but maintaining your new threads is something less thrilling. To save on dry cleaning costs, check to make sure garment is washable.

86. Forget air travel insurance. If you've charged your tickets to a major credit card, your loved ones will receive compensation in

the event of your unlikely demise.

87. Most men rent tuxedos when the occasion arises . . . why not women? Check out your community for party dress and bridal gown rental services and save hundreds of dollars for a real show stopper.

88. Once you've quit smoking you may need to lose weight. Doing both practically insures you will be sick less often (and at work) and cut medical costs.

89. Reuse Ziploc-type bags by washing them by hand or in the dishwasher, rinsing, and hanging them over various utensils in the dish drain. You'll save about $30 per year.

90. Free is the key. When your doctor prescribes a medication, ask if he or she has received any free samples of the drug from the pharmaceutical company (a common occurrence).

91. What's a movie without popcorn? A big savings, if you resist the concession prices. Bring your own snacks the next time you go.

92. There's no point in paying life insurance for life. Once your children are grown—and you're fifty and older—you should reconsider your policy.

93. Sometimes drastic measures are required. Keep the roof over your head by moving to a less expensive area.

94. Here's a routine saver, literally. Instead of squeezing toothpaste the full length of the toothbrush, just squeeze to the width of the brush. You'll be amazed how much longer a tube lasts!

95. You can't take it with you but you can leave it as you'd like. Have a recommended estate planning attorney draft your legal will and trust funds for a small fee. You may save your heirs bundles in taxes and probate fees.

96.   A country cottage, a ski chalet, a beachfront condo . . . all vacation homes, all money pits. Rent and enjoy for a week and leave the bills with the owner.

97.   Attention, dishwashers. Save 20 gallons of water by washing and rinsing in a dishpan or sink as opposed to letting the tap run. Save 13 gallons by using dishwasher short cycle, as opposed to the full cycle.

98.   Good neighbors make good resources: Share tools and ladders; trade special skills, such as tree pruning, cake decorating, throwing children's birthday parties, babysitting, plumbing, or nursing. The list is endless.

99.   Save 20 gallons of water each time you shower by wetting down first, turning off water to soap up, then turning back on to rinse off.

100.   Are high-priced sodas squeezing your grocery bill? Try a refreshing and healthier alternative: Take a slice of lemon, squeeze into a glass, and fill with ice and water.

101.   Save on heating costs this winter by opening curtains and shades in the morning (especially on windows with southern exposure) and closing them later in day to keep out cold.

102.   Pots of gold? When entertaining, consider hosting potluck dinners instead of more formal and expensive dinner parties.

103.   Try these energy savers. Make sure you don't block radiators and heating units with furniture and drapes. Close off rooms that are seldom used.

104.   Low-fat meals in one pot are good for your body and your budget. When possible, cook in pots on top of the stove instead of using the oven.

105.   Prolong the life of your car by getting regular oil changes (see

owner's manual for frequency). At that time check and fill, if necessary, brake and transmission fluids as well.

106. You'll add 10,000 to 15,000 miles to your automobile tires by making sure tire pressure is adjusted to recommended levels for summer and winter and that tires are rotated regularly (see owner's manual).

107. A variety (of homegrown herbs, that is) is the spice of life! They will grow well on a window sill or in a garden (many are perennials). Best of all, homegrown herbs taste better and are much cheaper than their supermarket counterparts.

108. Hotel rates are negotiable whether at the front desk or over the phone. You should know that corporate rates are not necessarily the lowest and weekend rates may apply one day before or after the weekend.

109. When planning trips with children look for accommodations where "kids stay free." Offers like this abound, especially during peak vacation times.

110. Here's a double whammy. Store coupons may be combined with manufacturer's coupons for tremendous savings.

111. This old saw is still humming: *Time is money.* When you're short on time you're more likely to eat out or buy expensive, processed foods, use a cleaning service, and buy costly gifts.

112. Memo to the dapper and chic: Don't buy any new clothes until you've paid for everything in your closet.

113. One trend of our decade is part-time employment. If you're looking for work, consider taking on two part-time jobs for a while.

114. Follow those garage sale signs to savings on room furnishings for your college student or first apartment.

115. Be cool and save. Research shows that window air conditioners are more energy efficient than central air. Common sense shows that fans are the best bet of all.

116. Supermarket savings may not meet the eye, literally. Look to the top shelves and also to the very bottom ones for maximum savings.

117. Memo to the trusting souls: Take time to review every bill for extra charges, especially those computer processed. You will be rewarded.

118. Just because you've declared independence from diapers doesn't mean throw them out. Cloth diapers make ideal dust cloths and last for years.

119. Here's yet another use for baking soda. Buy several boxes when on sale and use one cup in laundry in place of more expensive deodorizing/whitening products.

120. Cut out the fat (and save). Substitute applesauce for fats when making bread, cookies, and cakes. (It's even better if you make the applesauce yourself.)

121. Make long-distance calls after the sun goes down (when low rates start). Better yet, revive the lost art of letter writing.

122. Experience doesn't come cheap. Save on reupholstery by locating an upholstery school through the yellow pages.

123. A touch of lipstick can brighten any outfit or mood. Stretch each tube by applying with a small paintbrush, even when the tube is flat.

124. Enjoy window shopping. You don't have to buy something every time you go shopping.

125. Recycle not only the cereal box but also the liner inside. Wax paper liners can be used to line cake pans, roll out pie dough, or place between cuts of meat before freezing.

126. Cash for crude! Pay cash for gasoline and save up to 5 cents a gallon at many service stations. Use self-service pumps.

127. Cable television costs seem to escalate monthly. Save by reading the fine print in your contract to make sure you're not paying for unnecessary service. Compare costs of a rooftop antenna for long-term benefits.

128. When baking with glass or ceramic, lower the oven temperature 25 degrees. Baking time will remain the same.

129. Do you have a "dust bowl" in your home? Dusty silk flower arrangements can be quickly cleaned by washing them under the faucet. When they dry, they look just purchased.

130. Here's an old fiscal fiat: Before you pay any bills each month put some money into savings. If you wait until the bills are paid, forget it.

131. Be a person of the cloth . . . diapers and napkins, that is. Buy no-iron cloth napkins (or make your own) and realize big savings by laundering instead of disposing.

132. Comparison shopping applies to banks as well. Call local banks (and take notes) to find the ones with the lowest service charges and also those that pay interest on checking accounts.

133. Impulse buying is seldom financially responsible. Having said this, resist television shopping clubs.

134. Wall-to-wall or nothing at all? Achieve the look of carpeting by purchasing a carpet remnant and having it bound.

135. The best rates on car loans are usually available from credit unions. Rates may be as much as two percentage points lower.

136. Stop trying to impress people. You'll save thousands, literally.

137. Shop—not until you drop—but only when you need something. Almost 70 percent of adults go to a mall each week and probably have credit crises to match.

138. Wear things out. Before resigning an item to the Salvation Army or the trash, ask if there might be another use for it.

139. Elbow grease saves money (a statement for our time!). Wash and vacuum your car yourself and save at least $6 each time. Better, have your kids or young neighbors take on the job . . . and still save.

140. Wait until you hear this: Wait until you have the money before you buy something.

141. Expensive purchases that will last forever but will outlast your purposes are to be shunned.

142. When you see the dress you've always wanted or the sweater to die for . . . wait. Go back in a few weeks and chances are you'll be able to buy it on sale.

143. Do it yourself, or *learn* to do it yourself. Prepare your own taxes, bake a cake from scratch, sew a pair of pants, fix a leaky faucet . . . *ad* nauseam, but the savings *add* up.

144. Be in the know. Even if your bank offers free ATM service, you can be charged up to $2 per transaction at another bank's machine.

145. The bridal aisle should be strewn with petals, not ungainly bills. Consider brunch food as opposed to dinner fare; rural locations, college halls, parks, church fellowship halls, and home weddings; and your own homegrown flowers.

146. Don't fritter away your pension benefits by changing jobs too

frequently.

147. Don't be misled by the grace periods on credit cards. Grace periods only apply if you paid your previous month's bill in full.

148. It may not look like much . . . . Maintain your car for a minimum of five years (and preferably longer) instead of buying a new one. You'll save on insurance and monthly payments.

149. If you have an automatic dishwasher, stop it before the drying cycle, open the door, and let the dishes air dry. Every penny counts.

150. Old cars don't necessarily die, but they sure don't require collision coverage. Review your policy if your car is five years old (or older).

151. How does an inexpensive lithograph become a gallery masterpiece? By having it framed, of course, and paying through the nose. Try using "do-it-yourself" frame shops and save.

152. In the category of you've heard this before . . . . When considering home repairs, get several bids.

153. Try selling your home yourself. You'll save several thousand dollars in realtor commissions, but it's not easy.

154. Refinance your mortgage. If rates drop 2 percent below your current rate (or more), the time is now.

155. Are you wasting watts? Turn off the television and all lights when you're not in the room.

156. Be in the know for less. Instead of subscribing to one or more newspapers or magazines, split the cost of subscriptions with a neighbor.

157. Pressure cookers conjure up negative images, unless you're

thinking of the time-saving stove-top meat tenderizer! The toughest parts of meat can be tenderized in minutes and food cooked in one-half to one-third the usual time.

158. If you pop a button, put it in a safe place (and sew on later). You'll keep your clothes longer.

159. When purchasing furniture or appliances you'll save by buying floor models. Only you will know the difference.

160. We've become a catalog culture and savings are to be had in some instances. Learn to compare in-store with mail-order prices.

161. It's your money. Whenever any purchase fails to meet your expectations, return it.

162. "Some assembly required." These are not famous last words when it comes to furniture . . . you'll reap big savings.

163. Wax efficient! If you freeze candles before using them, you'll add hours to an enchanted evening.

164. Produce marked "3 for $1.00" doesn't mean you have to buy three. Buy one for only 34 cents!

165. Who needs a Shylock? Resist borrowing money from a friend and ruining a perfectly fine friendship.

166. A healthy marriage is an incalculable financial (and, of course, personal) asset. Romancing your spouse doesn't have to be costly.

167. After you've raked (and raked) those leaves, let them work for you. Put leaves in a compost bin and next spring you'll have free mulch and fertilizer to be worked into the garden.

168. You work hard for your money. Don't throw it away buying lottery tickets.

169. Let's do lunch . . . and save? Brown bag it to work and save at least a mortgage payment a year.

170. The fastest way up the corporate ladder may be in the classroom. Check out the possibility of tuition assistance courtesy of your employer.

171. Here's another shortcut up the corporate ladder: Even if you're in the proverbial mailroom, look for ways for your employer to cut costs.

172. Work out of your home if you start your own business. You'll be off to a better start.

173. Live close to where you work. You'll save on tolls, gasoline, and car maintenance, not to mention your equilibrium.

174. Save the four-star feasts for special occasions. Even then, stay clear of the overhyped, expensive restaurants in favor of smaller establishments without liquor licenses.

175. Culinary caveat no. 2: Pass up the dessert cart and have a treat at home. All right, share a dessert then.

176. Culinary caveat no. 3: Know the prices of today's specials, heretofore unspoken, before ordering one.

177. Trim your Christmas tree without taking a chunk out of your holiday budget. Make your own decorations or, if you have children, watch as they bring home new ones from school each year.

178. You don't have to be "crafty" to make a Christmas wreath. Trim a few boughs from the base of your tree and shape into a wreath, holding everything together with green wire. Garnish with holiday ribbon.

179. Bed and breakfast inns are not for everyone but for uniqueness, comfort, and satisfying food and fare, they can't be beat.

(For more information check out *The Christian Bed and Breakfast Directory,* Barbour Books.)

180. A security deposit, literally? If you're collecting social security, ask that your checks be deposited directly into your checking account.

181. You've led a modest life and in keeping with that you'd probably like a modest funeral. Your family may feel differently after you die. Prepay funeral costs while you're still alive and put all requests for the service itself in writing.

182. F.Y.I.: File away warranties and owner's manuals in one location in your home. One week before the warranty expires, you may need to make some repairs.

183. Pasta dishes are inexpensive and delicious, and besides that, kids almost universally crave them. Make them low fat as well as economical by reducing fat in recipe: Use less than required amounts of butter and cheese (use Romano instead of Parmesan) and use low-fat milk when making sauces.

184. Serve meatless dinners occasionally, for your budget and your health.

185. If you're apartment hunting, make every effort to find your new digs without a broker's assistance.

186. Unless you're in a coupon trading club, cut only those coupons you'll use. A coupon caveat: Make sure you can't buy another brand for less.

187. Never visit a supermarket on an empty stomach. You know why.

188. You may have to squint to read the unit prices at the supermarket but it's worth it. Actual prices do not necessarily reveal the best values.

189. Lightweight wools and other medium-weight fabrics may be worn

yearround. Begin investing in such a wardrobe, especially if your job requires a polished look.

190. Patience is always a virtue. Wait until the end of the month to shop for important items, household and otherwise. (This also holds true when shopping for a car.) Quotas need to be met and bargains can be had.

191. Old broom and mop handles have a legion of uses. Paintbrush extenders, garden stakes, and costume props are a few.

192. Ship books via fourth-class mail (book rate). In fact, eschew first-class mail for most packages.

193. More options on a car usually mean more things to go wrong. Concentrate on the essentials when wheeling and dealing.

194. Welcome hand-me-down toys from friends and relatives. The toys have lasted this long (i.e., they're not junk) and you'll save a swingset on such generosity.

195. Used computer paper and the backs of school bulletins and worksheets make great paper for coloring and craft projects. Unfortunately, most fax paper won't work as well.

196. Save a life and unnecessary expense. Select your next pet (with a small donation) at your local animal shelter.

197. Animal lovers make great relatives and friends. When you have to leave town, find one to housesit Muffin and save on kennel fees, sometimes starting at $10 per day for small animals.

198. Don't wait until disaster strikes. Make sure your homeowner's insurance is up to date with the current value of your home.

199. God is your loving Heavenly Father and He wants you to be happy. Take your worries to the Lord and live each day within your means . . .for Him.

Guarantee

If you read this book and apply the principles contained in it, you will save at least 100 times what you paid for it or we will refund the purchase price. Tear off front cover and return with sales receipt and name and address of bookstore to the following address: BCI, P.O. Box 719, Uhrichsville, Ohio 44683.